BOOK AT US NOW

CORONET

First published in Great Britain in 2011 by Coronet
An imprint of Hodder & Stoughton
An Hachette UK company

3

A CIP catalogue record for this title is available from the British Library

ISBN 978 1 444 72928 3

Printed and bound in Spain by Cayfosa Impresia Iberica S.A

Design by www.envydesign.co.uk

Hodder & Stoughton policy is to use papers that are natural, renewable and
recyclable products and made from wood grown in sustainable forests. The logging
and manufacturing processes are expected to conform to the environmental
regulations of the country of origin.

Hodder & Stoughton Ltd
338 Euston Road
London NW1 3BH

www.hodder.co.uk

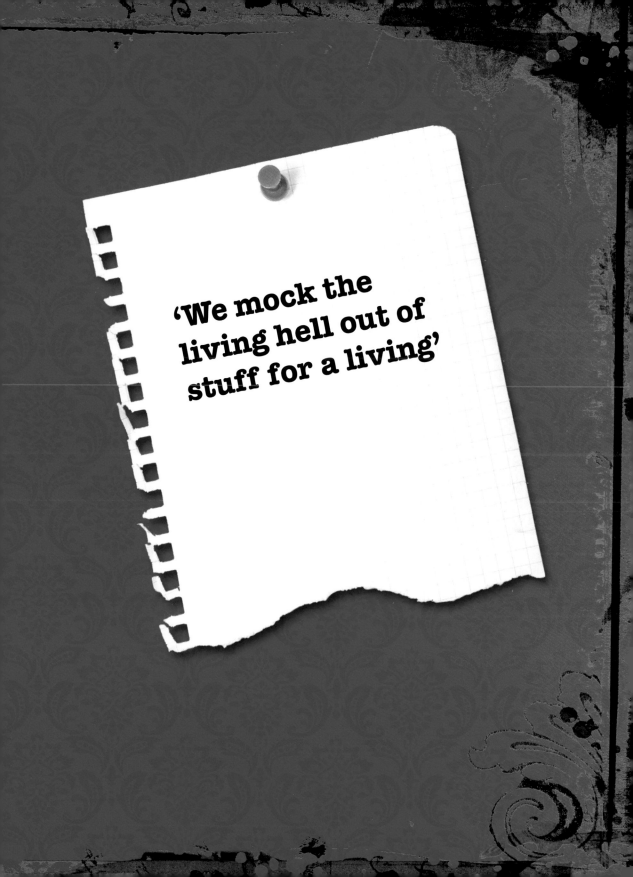

STEFAN

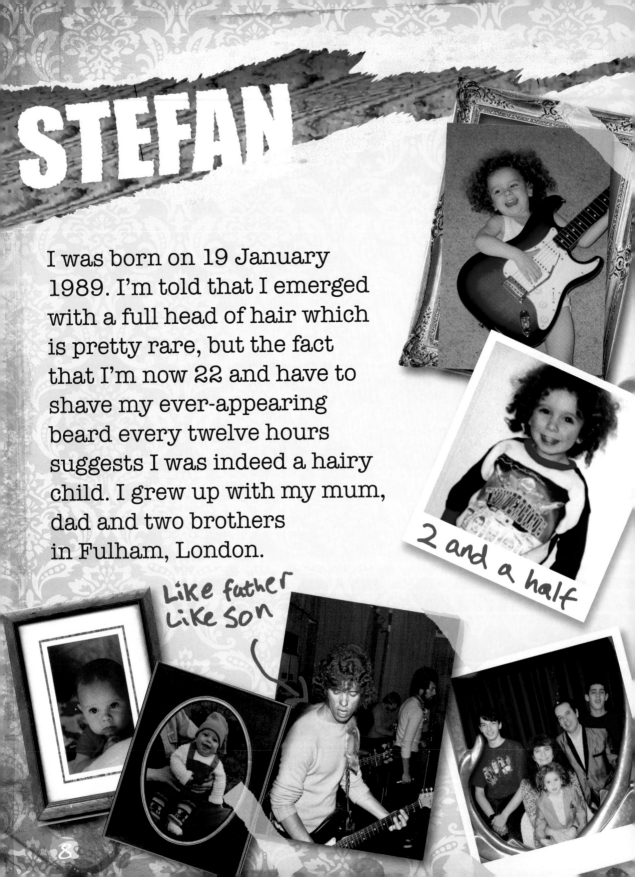

I was born on 19 January 1989. I'm told that I emerged with a full head of hair which is pretty rare, but the fact that I'm now 22 and have to shave my ever-appearing beard every twelve hours suggests I was indeed a hairy child. I grew up with my mum, dad and two brothers in Fulham, London.

2 and a half

Like father like son

My brother Kyle – who is now our DJ – used to play a lot of dance music. I would run around to it in his room, whilst his friends would make me say 'ACIIIIIIIIIID' and do the running man. I also had blond dreadlocks at the time, which I guess made it even funnier for them. My parents played (and still do) in a band, which I grew up watching. Normally when they'd do a show my brother Tcha would look after me. He used to let me stay up late and watch *Jackass* or *South Park* and play on his Nintendo, blasting aliens' heads off. Those years were fun because nothing else mattered apart from blowing stuff up.

I started piano lessons when I was six but thought it was shit and for shit people that couldn't play the guitar. My dad insisted it was the best instrument, so I carried on long enough to get asked to leave by my piano teacher – that's right, she refused to carry on taking money from me – because I never practised.

Then came my obsession with musicals (what?). I appeared in *Oliver!* at the London Palladium (during which I literally wet my trousers), *Whistle Down the Wind* at the Aldwych with the now famous Jessie J (she was the first girl I ever saw kiss a boy with tongues) and *Tess of the D'Urbervilles* (yes, they made a musical of it; yes, it had a song about rape in it; and yes, it got shut down immediately). So by the age of ten I was a musical-theatre has-been, known around the industry for pissing my pants and closing shows down ... It was time to learn the electric make-girls-scream guitar.

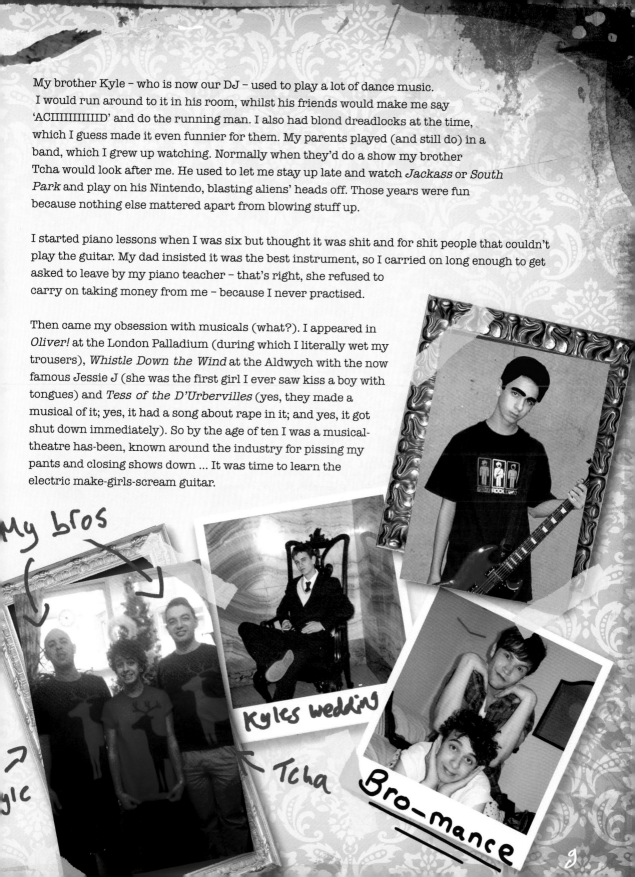

My bros

Kyles wedding

Tcha

Bro-mance

yle

Ashley Horne

I met Ashley Neil Horne break-dancing in a nursery rhymes video when I was 12 (more on that later), which coincidentally left me with a hernia and a week off school playing Metal Gear Solid 2 on PlayStation. Ashley and I shared a love for Warhammer 40k – you know, those little figures that all the boys at school paint then don't do anything with? Yeah, those boys were us. Ashley had Orcs and I was Space Marines (but I couldn't paint so my mum did all that for me – don't tell Ashley). To this day Ash still keeps his Warhammer shit in some kind of pervert cabinet in his room ... but he'll deny that.

Ashley Horne used to come round my house every Thursday after school to play Tony Hawks and talk about ~~boys~~ girls. We both thought the idea of learning guitar was cool and luckily my dad could play so he agreed to give us lessons. Ashley got bored straight away but surprisingly I was interested. The next week I started a pop-punk band called Ink with a girl drummer (yes, girls *can* play the drums?!?!!!) and a boy from school on the big guitar. We started holding shows/parties at the local community centre, which of course led to under-age drinking, under-age foreplay, under-age drug use and someone getting headbutted ... After a couple of weeks the dream of giving local kids a chance to

How small is Ash?!

Party Boy!

First Rehearsal

10

hang out was dead. But my dream of getting into local girls' beds was not, so I kept playing in my band however and wherever I could. Let's get one thing straight: at the age of 12 the only reason I started playing music was to get attention from girls, and at the age of 22 I'd be lying if I said it wasn't still: IT ACTUALLY WORKS!

So the girls liked me but boys on the other hand usually hated me. I remember we built a website for my band at the time and some nerds from another school made a clone website with pictures of men jacking off into my ears and stuff like that ... I thought it was funny but none of our parents agreed.

Dru Wakely

I then met Dru Wakely on a drama summer camp. He was older than me and went to a rough school so it was a safe bet hanging out with him. At the time my ex-girlfriend was off doing whatever 14-year-olds do

1. Dru's Famous Finger

2. There it is again.....

3. And again....

Look how big these drums are!

11

with another boy, so Dru helped nurse my wounded soul and put up with listening to my heartbroken songs. He actually really liked them and wanted to play drums in my band, the only problem being he didn't have any drums and had never played before, so I made him do an audition on a wooden box he found in the street. And he was really good (I think!), which meant we HAD to start a band. As soon as we got home we formed Icarus Burning with a boy called Simon from a posh school. I taught myself how to scream like all the bands were doing back then and we started getting booked to play REAL venues with REAL audience members and REAL house parties with REAL girls.

When I was 15 Ashley, me and a few more boys from class were assigned to make a short film for our Expressive Arts project; we chose to recreate some scenes from *Saving Private Ryan* (which I had never seen, but had heard was quite good) in a forest in Barnes. We went a bit crazy with the ketchup, so the passers-by who witnessed four boys dressed as soldiers and covered in fake blood stumbling out of a forest are probably still talking about it now. But NO, you are not allowed to see it. We knew how to press record on our camera but had no clue what to do with the footage after that. I'd heard of editing before so I took it upon myself to learn ... And for some reason, I was hooked. I made loads of stupid films with my school friends (they are probably on YouTube) and even a couple of music videos. Unlike music, though, editing does not get you girl-attention, so I made sure to keep a good balance between the two.

For some reason, at this stage of my life (maybe due to the chokers, studs, chains and blue hair) I started getting mugged a lot – in fact everyone did. It was a regular occurrence to get chased by a gang of hooded boys wielding fireworks and blasting rap out of a shitty little speaker on their mobile phone. This somehow introduced me to rap music and as a joke I wrote a song about my favourite trainers at the time, my white Nike dunks. For some reason it started getting me attention. I came second in the BBC's hunt for the Best Band in the World and I came first in Diesel's hunt for the Best Urban Act in the UK. The track was even used in the film *Adulthood* in an oral sex scene between Danny Dyer and some unfortunate woman. The band name I put that out under was The Clik Clik and we sold 500 copies of our first single, which was released on vinyl (you can't put them in your computer). We supported Alphabeat, Lethal Bizzle, Crystal Castles and Hadouken on tour, and we even nearly got signed. But then I'd probably be in a band like the The Ting Tings, so if anything I'm kind of glad that didn't happen (no offence Stacey... or is it Jane? No, that's not her name).

The Beast begins ...

Like all good stories, ours begins with a party. In Summer 2009, Dru Wakely and I went to a friend's birthday, but little did we know this party would flick a switch inside of our heads that would trigger something ridiculously exciting. It was a good party, but the entry fee on the door was laughable and the drinks were expensive – so expensive that we took to inventing a game called Minesweeping (turn to page 47 for the rules) – not like that shitty game on your PC. This game involved seeing a drink left unattended, picking it up and drinking it ... simple. Two days later it was inspiration enough for us to write a song called 'Ninjas', about the very same thing. We had a middle bit in that song about Snoop Dogg, a bit that we knew neither of us could do. We needed someone with a voice as awkward as his eyebrows, and that man was Ashley Neil Horne.

He was gonna come round and record the vocals for 'Ninjas' but I heard a song on YouTube that gave me an idea: what if we took a song already big enough to get us some attention, changed the words and put that up first? That song was 'Tik Tok' by a girl called Ke$ha, a song so fucking catchy you couldn't shake it off your ears inside a jet engine. I remember the first time I heard it I was glued to my seat by the lyrics, and was already scribbling words in my notebook excitedly. I went online and told Dru and Ash my plan for world domination (to me back then the world was 100 people and domination was making half of them laugh a bit ... little did I know the world was much bigger than that, luckily for me).

I started writing and recording all the vocals underneath my bunk bed in my 'home studio' but it was missing something: a bridge. At this point Ashley wasn't fully committed to making an arse out of himself for the world to see, so the team was still only two men strong. Dru popped round to help me finish the track and thought for some reason it'd be a good idea to copy 'Lose Yourself' by Eminem in the bridge – you know, that bit that goes 'This is the part where the rap breaks down' and he was right ... SO WE DID!

Dru had a pretty dark past so we threw a bit in there about his dad leaving him on Christmas Eve and BOOM the song was done.

On 13 December Ashley decided he was in. If not vocally he was at least willing to bring along his best dance moves. So he got the train to Fulham (where I live) from smelly Reading (where he lives) and we proceeded to dance around in swimming trunks and vest tops in my parents house which from now on will be named Abingdon Mansions. And man did we sweat. I imported all the footage into my computer straight after and proceeded to edit like a crazy man until 3am. It was 14 December and we were ready to create a YouTube account. Me and Dru had been dicking around making electro beats with live drums and were about to start DJ'ing under the name The Midnight Beast. We decided that was never going to happen so instead we used the name for our YouTube page. To this day I am so happy we chose something so memorable instead of FISHMAN1001 or something.

GO

YOUR VIDEO HAS NOW BEEN UPLOADED TO YOUTUBE.

Abingdon Studios

TIK TOK

We were so pleased with ourselves we started sending it to all of our Facebook friends, getting them to post it on each other's walls. We were superstars, megastars, more famous than our wildest dreams ... WE HAD 75 FUCKINGGGGG VIEWSSSSSSS!!!!!!!!!! What? Only 75 views? Oh ... And then suddenly came an avalanche of attention as the Internet turned its head to check out The Midnight Beast ... Ke$ha went to number one in every country in the flipping world and did all of our advertising for us ... We just sat back and watched the views roll in. Perez Hilton was tweeting about us, Shane Dawson was tweeting about us and even KE$HA was tweeting about us ...

'HOLY SHIT! THIS IS BETTER THAN MY VERSION'

GO

yep

On Christmas Day a week later we had 250,000 views and were front page of MTV.com ... And pretty soon after that came a million hits on YouTube and a number one on iTunes Australia. How's that for a Christmas present?

I'm 22 years old which means that I've blown out exactly 253 candles on my cake (that's if every single birthday cake I've received has had my exact age of candles) ... What I'm trying to say is that's a lot of wishes and I've never once wished to be an Internet sensation famous for prancing around my parents' house in a T-shirt more colourful than monster vomit ... but I'm grateful.

The next thing to do was ride that wave for a while so we made 'XXXMas Buddies' and 'Down', which were both parodies, but that was the easy part: no one's gonna win an award for ripping apart someone else's tune. Now it's do-or-die, original material, our own words, our own music ... But we weren't even worried, we had 'Ninjas' up our sleeve and a brand-new idea all about lesbians.

When fame strikes

One of the first crazy things that happened for the three of us was going to the Cobra Starship show. We hadn't yet played our own first show so even though we'd seen millions of hits on YouTube we didn't really know if they were all just from a couple of perverts on the other side of the world. Gabe from Cobra Starship liked our stuff and invited us to come along and watch their show. We figured it might be a good idea to sit in the Royal Box ... better view, and well, we're royalty right? We arrived late so the crowd was already formed. As soon as we took our seats the whole of the Shepherds Bush Empire turned to look at us and proceeded to sing our 'Tik Tok' parody ... it was one of the most bizarre things any of us has ever experienced. Suddenly we realised how many people had heard of us. If this was just one room, what about all the others?

What?

Cool hair!

My first Demo

16

SEX?

IN THE STUDIO, BY STEFAN

Unlike most bands we do not record in a big state-of-the-art studio in central London. Instead we record underneath the bunk bed that my brother built me, in my parents' house in Fulham.

Budget

bra

bra

Messy

THE PERFECT SLEEPOVER

When life gets too much, the best thing to do is invite your friends round, slip on your jimmy jammies, get comfortable and snack out watching a *Sex and the City* box set. But if you don't have the brainpower to put together the perfect sleepover yourself ... read on.

You will need:

At least one person (it helps if you know them)
Sex and the City box set
Some classic films (*Notebook*, *Brokeback Mountain*, *Legally Blonde*, etc)
One box of tissues (for heartbroken tears)
Some face masks
A camera (FOR FACEBOOK LOL!!!)

You will play:

Spin the bottle
Twister
Kiss chase
Pin the tail on the donkey
Who's got the biggest bum?

You will have:

The best night of your life!!!!!!!!

You smiling ↙

Stef's floor

VO GUE!!

A$hLey woz ere!!

STUSSY!

what's he covering?

19

ASHLEY'S GUIDE TO
SOCIAL ETIQUETTE FOR ALL OCCASIONS

You've come to the master of social skills. You want to be like me? No doubt. Who wouldn't want my amazing personality? Obviously no one, because if you didn't want to be like me then you're a loser and you probably spend your days sat at home watching reruns of *Star Trek*. Booya. I will now spill all my secrets on how to be the best at life situations. Are you ready for this jelly? OK. LET'S GO, BITCHEZZZZ.

Chatting up ~~girls~~ ~~boys~~ ~~girls~~ ~~boys~~ GIRLS!!!

You're in a bar and you see a well fit bird, she gives you the eye – you know, the 'come over here and bang me' look. First impressions are important so you must walk over to her with a confident bounce in your stride. Girls dig bad boys so don't smile once, look at her as if you wanna smack her one. No need for small talk, just chuck her one of these dirty lines and she will be joining you for a party in your pants:

1. How do you like your eggs? Poached, scrambled, or fertilised?

2. Sit on my lap and let's talk about the first thing that pops up.

3. Are you breaking wind? Because you are blowing me away.

4. You wearing mirrored underwear? Cos I can see myself in it.

5. I'm guessing your legs are like Tesco ... open 24 hours a day.

6. My watch says you're naked. Oh, you're not? My watch must be an hour fast. (Oh yeah.)

7. I'm a great swimmer, how about I do some breaststroke?

8. I wish you were a door so I could bang you all night long.

9. Roses are red, violets are blue, I suck at poems. Nice tits.

10. Love, get your coat ... I have a concealed weapon.

Talking to a Princess or Queen

You're in a bar and you see a well fit princess or queen. Now, I'm telling you from past experience, do not stride over unless you are in the correct garms. I suggest you find yourself a robe, sceptre and a golden crown (Toys R Us, £4.99). She will now give you the acknowledgement you deserve. Get her drunk off a few bottles of champagne and you should have a one-way ticket to Sex in the City. It works every time. PLAYAAA ;)

Cinema Etiquette

Some sexy bitch has asked you out on a date to see a movie. Make sure you pick a film with no hope in hell of being entertaining or compelling. It will just damage your chances of mouth to mouth action. Giggidy. She wants a large popcorn and a large Coke. You don't want your girl getting a fat ass, so hit her with this line, it works every time: 'Babes, it might be in your best interest not to go for this option, you could do with losing a few pounds.' She will respect you big time for looking out for her weight.

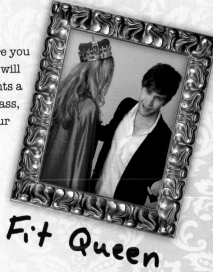

Fit Queen

The cinema will be very dark, so if you want to get cheeky cheeky, you can. Don't worry about everyone else viewing the movie, they will be considerate to your situation. HIGH FIVE.

School Reunions

You open a letter to reveal an invite to a secondary-school reunion. Do you go? YES YES YES. It's a great way to show off what accomplishments you have achieved in life. Prepare for the occasion by doing the following:

1. Hire a smoking-hot female escort. Pretend she is your wife/girlfriend, or even your mistress, you will gain much more respect for that.

2. Wear a sparkly silver suit and a trilby. People will think you have loads of money. A gold suit, however, is a big no-no, it's just tacky.

3. When the peasants ask the dreaded question, 'So what do you do?' make sure you have a bad-ass job title ready. ' I am a Ninja-Secret-Agent-Vampire-Billionaire' – that should do the trick.

Any other social situation

Just talk about yourself, do not listen to others. Remember, there is no one more important than YOU. Good luck in life, not that you are gonna need it. Boom.

AN-DRU

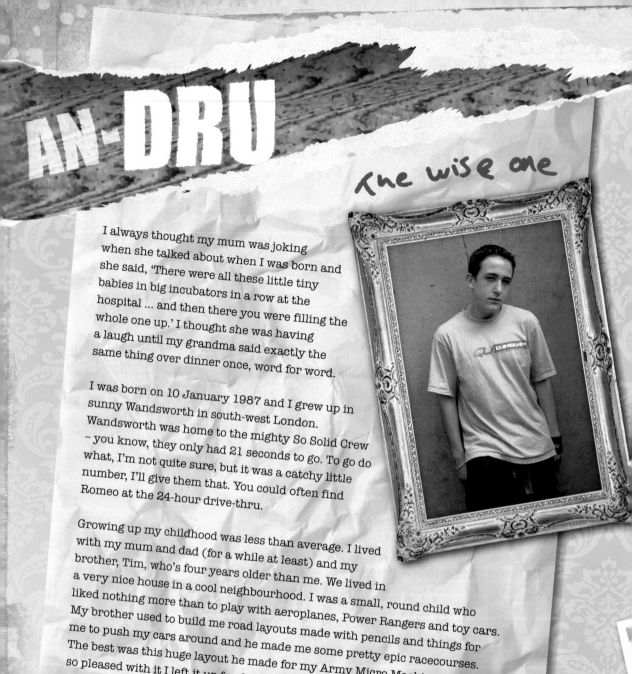

I always thought my mum was joking when she talked about when I was born and she said, "There were all these little tiny babies in big incubators in a row at the hospital ... and then there you were filling the whole one up." I thought she was having a laugh until my grandma said exactly the same thing over dinner once, word for word.

I was born on 10 January 1987 and I grew up in sunny Wandsworth in south-west London. Wandsworth was home to the mighty So Solid Crew – you know, they only had 21 seconds to go. To go do what, I'm not quite sure, but it was a catchy little number, I'll give them that. You could often find Romeo at the 24-hour drive-thru.

Growing up my childhood was less than average. I lived with my mum and dad (for a while at least) and my brother, Tim, who's four years older than me. We lived in a very nice house in a cool neighbourhood. I was a small, round child who liked nothing more than to play with aeroplanes, Power Rangers and toy cars. My brother used to build me road layouts made with pencils and things for me to push my cars around and he made me some pretty epic racecourses. The best was this huge layout he made for my Army Micro Machines and I was so pleased with it I left it up for days. The sweet and harmless cars and planes were soon replaced with playing 007 on our Nintendo 64, and killing each other with a golden gun. Tim was crap so I used to win all the time. We'd play for hours.

Now, you're probably thinking, what's not normal about that?

Well there weren't always just the four of us playing happy families. While I was growing up, sometimes there were actually five of us in the house. My mum had hired a cleaner to help with the chores. At the time she seemed nice. She was Spanish, pretty friendly but not particularly fit by any means. If anything, she had a bit of a hairy lip. Now if a boy of six years old can notice that there is hair on a lady where it shouldn't be, you know it's got to be bad. Hairy lip or not, little did I know that this bitch was about to turn my world upside down.

It's true

It was a cold dark Christmas Eve when my dad popped out for some milk. When I think about it now, we should have known that the shops would have been closed already for the Christmas break, but I was too busy shouting after him, asking him to bring me back a Twix, to notice. Days passed with no Twix and no milk. There was absolutely no sign whatsoever of my dad. I think it was after a week or so that I started to put two and two together. Our cleaner hadn't returned after the weekend either. The final light-bulb moment that made me think something might be up was when I found my mum staring at a burning bin in the garden. I could
 see my dad's things poking out as the flames grew higher. My mum was just standing there, staring at it, clutching a bottle of Jack in her hand. I ran upstairs to my room to do the same, only I was clutching a bottle of Calpol instead of Jack Daniels and I skipped the bit with the burning bin.

From then on life was far from OK. My early teenage years were a fine blend of drunken brawls, unsuccessful robbery attempts and casual sex. Not to mention me drinking my weight in Calpol over the years. I told myself that I liked to think of it as a nightcap. I must have single-handedly kept that company in business.

Me + My boy
Ashley.G.

Early TMB

Perfect People

** I AM OBLIGED TO TELL YOU THAT I DO NOT CONDONE DRUGS AND STRONGLY ADVISE YOU NOT TO CASUALLY DRINK CALPOL**

All of this led to anger issues, casual yet blunt spurts of profanity and in my darkest hour, in need of a Calpol fix, I tried to hold up my local chemist ...

From then on things changed for me. I'd been to a great primary school and had a real laugh with my friends but when I moved to secondary school, I found it was rough as fuck. It was like a stereotypical shit school:

Fights – A daily occurrence

Fire - Once

Blood drawn - Sometimes

Old-school male teacher who casually chewed tobacco - Always

Younger hot female teacher who was preyed upon by the hormonal boys - Sadly yes, though not by me, just so that we're clear.

The dodgy career advice handed out by teachers who didn't think playing drums was a career – Yeah there was a fair bit of that too, but look at me now biatch!

What really kept me sane were the friends I made outside the school gates.
I met another friend called Ashley, who is basically a brother from another mother to me,
at the same acting class where I would meet Stefan a couple of years later. In the meantime,
at school I found comfort in a small group of friends who shared with me a love for skateboarding
and music. We were named the grunger or skater kids and everyone thought we listened to nothing
but Slipknot and other death/screamo bands. I wasn't even a fan of Slipknot. I didn't really care
what the others thought and my favourite memory was on my last day there when this kid came
up to me. He thought he was the toughest boy in the school but he wasn't at all by far. He looked
and me and said, 'Safe Andrew, sorry about all the bullying, yeah?' I was amazed: he hadn't
bullied me at all. I told him as much and he looked pretty disappointed. What a DOUCHE!

NINJAS OF THE DANCE FLOOR!

Mr Stefan Abingdon and myself somehow got invited to a party at this *cough* 'exclusive' club. Now you may have noticed the way I've just written 'exclusive' with what would be a dry, sarky cough if this were audio. This is because it was one of those annoying clubs. You know, the ones that charge something silly on the door and usually won't allow you in unless you're wearing some smart shoes that you'd wear if you were still at school or the ones some parents make their kids wear to church. Luckily, though, through friends we made it on a 'free list', woo!

Although we escaped the hefty entry fee we couldn't avoid how much the drinks cost. Mental amounts. I think we both stuck to purchasing one each. We had to buy at least one, we didn't want to look tight or anything. But neither of us wanted to pay that much again so we knew we had to do something both cunning and drastic. The result was 'Minesweeping':

Minesweeping: - the activity of detecting and disposing of ~~marine mines.~~ unattended drinks to get as drunk as possible for free!

Now before you start to wonder, Ashley Neil Horne was at home in Reading but YES we were all in each other's lives already and YES we were all friends. You'll just read more about that later on ...

Minesweeping soon became a friendly competition where we pretty ~~uch~~ congratulated each other on pinching drinks from different tables: ~~ine~~ swoop there,' 'Lovely steal.'

~~s~~ a successful night and now feeling like ninjas we ~~elt~~ inspired to tell our tale in the form of a rap. ~~ed~~ us to write 'Ninjas', primarily ~~o.~~ Yes,

AT THIS POINT (ALREADY) IN THE BOOK I'AM NOW OBLIGED TO TELL YOU ON BEHALF OF THE MIDNIGHT BEAST THAT WE DO NOT CONDONE ~~THEFT, DRINKING, OBSCENE DANCING AND PROFANITY.*~~

*paying high entry fees, being forced to wear smart shoes!

Snoop - Nob

Drunk - Again

27

crazily and shockingly, in its, er, birth, I guess, The Midnight Beast was not quite a trio (although Stefan's hair can count as its own person when it's left to grow). But fear not because – well actually, let's face it, you know we all end up working together. (And that has saved me writing another paragraph! *rubs hands together*.)

So a few months later, with the song 'Ninjas' already in the bag, Stefan, Ashley and me were all going nuts about the latest Call of Duty game and were too busy playing online together to care about anything else. Yes that's right, we geek out online. While I'm winning like there's no tomorrow, Stefan starts to tell us (over our headsets) about this new song he's heard by Ke$ha called 'Tik Tok'. He said he'd had a brainwave about being cheeky and changing her 'under-average' lyrics to slightly better, more comedic ones by, let's say, some 'under-average guys' – see what I did there? Anyway Ashley and I both found the prospect of this parody hilarious but while I was arranging with Stefan when to go round and help him finish off the lyrics, Ash wasn't quite ready to give up the life of a serious actor. Nor was he ready to just hop on the bloody train from Reading to Fulham either.

It wasn't really until the song was recorded and we were thinking of some crazy shit to do in an extremely low-fi video that Ashley was fully prepared to share his crazy-ass dance skills and strange-yet-comical facial expressions. He also liked the fact he could bare his arms in a vest top, too.

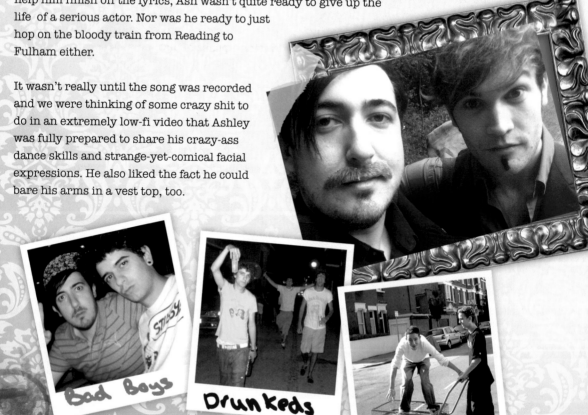

Bad Boys

Drunkeds

Jackass

Stefan Abingdon and Ashley Horne

I should probably take it back now to how we all met each other. Mr Stefan and Mr Ashley both went to the same theatre school but actually met on the set of some nursery rhyme video. I think the guy was called Dave Benson Phillips – look it up online and try to spot them. I haven't yet seen it myself, mainly because I couldn't be arsed to search. After this first encounter with each other they became inseparable buddies and went on to perform in plays together, audition for adverts (FACT: Stefan was the voice for the animated Milky Bar kid, and Ash was the *Daily Express* delivery voice) and even star as extras in *Harry Potter* (I think Stef did the voiceover for the owl and Ash was Hermione's stunt double). The pair also made some lovely home-made short films. That just sounds awful so let me just very quickly add that it wasn't porn, but merely remakes of such classic films as *Saving Private Ryan*. They also couldn't get enough of that game Warhammer either.

Now, as if Stef wasn't getting enough from stage school, he decided to join a drama class, the same one that I was already attending. I met Stef there when I was about 14 and he was about 12 and literally the day we met we pretty much made a band. We got talking and one of the first things he asked me was if I

played anything. I'd sort of just started to play drums and by that I mean I frantically air drummed along to Blink 182 and had the odd lesson at school. Stefan said he wanted to start a band so the following day I went and got a kit. Makes sense right? We've pretty much played in bands together since that day.

So to summarise, Ashley and Stef geeked out over Warhammer and Stef and I geeked out over music and bands! Fuck me, we're cool, aren't we?

But this now leaves the important link between Mr Ashley Neil Horne and myself. Our friendship was warmly invited by Stef and was a gradually blossoming one at that. I met him during a phase of his where he constantly did David Brent impressions, badly, and to make it worse he did them in his unbroken voice. 'I don't agree with that in the workplace.' Looking back on it, it was actually quite hilarious.

Ash would basically come down to the gigs where Stef and I played and soon became our favourite and trusted groupie. He was such a good groupie we invited him and another good friend of ours out to Ibiza where we had been given a residency slot at the Ibiza Rocks Hotel.

So this particular trip away may have been the start of a spiralling end to the band Stef and I were in, but it was certainly the start of the trio's friendship.

sober?

clik-clik

Beefa '09

Kissy

DJ set......

THE MIDNIGHT BEAST ANSWER LIFE'S TEN BIGGEST QUESTIONS

Life has many questions and people have always tried but failed to answer them. Luckily this trio of haphazard comedians know way more than your favourite scientist. Here are life's biggest questions answered by The Midnight Beast.

Why is the sky blue, Ashley?
Because blue is my favorite colour, thanks God!

Where do we go after we die, Stefan?
Usually the ground or a giant oven ... or sometimes limbo, which is apparently just like Ibiza.

What makes grass green, Dru?
Because green is my favorite colour, thanks God!

Why do fish live in the sea, Stefan?
Everybody knows that fish are a super-race hatching a plan to take over the world from underneath the ground, gradually nibbling beneath pavements and floorboards ready to drown us all in a slow painful death.

And why don't fish have legs, Ashley?
Because they're lazy.

Why are we here, Dru?
To write a book.

Where do babies come from, Stefan?
Mum said a stork carries them down from his big stork's nest and hands them to loving parents all around the world. I believe her because I'm her baby.

Why do men have nipples, Dru?
Why should women have all the fun? It's like masturbating but not as messy.

Why can't men get pregnant, Ashley?
Because they have no womb for a baby.

What came first, Stefan, the chicken or the egg?
The predicament this question leaves most people in is if the *egg* came before the chicken then what laid the egg? Simple. The thought of a chicken laying an egg is ridiculous.

Hello Ladies

DOWN

This video was filmed at my uncle's house... ↘ M3 cor

SUPERHEROES TMB STYLE

We've been known to dress up as superheroes on occasion (we're just a bunch of nerds), but that being said, a superhero doesn't always have to be super. Here's some supershit heroes that we came up with for your viewing pleasure:

Introducing Soup-a-man
Name: SOUP-A-MAN
Alias: Barry Smith

Sent to Earth by his father to save the human race after his planet was destroyed by an evil Soup-a-villain, Soup-a-man found rental prices high and so applied for a job at the local soup kitchen, harnessing his powers to what he knows best ... making soup. Although a mild-mannered character, if you get on the wrong side of him he's been known to throw mildly hot soup at you. Although it won't burn, it will feel really annoying and be hard to get out of white clothes: this can be an inconvenience to Soup-a-villains all over planet Earth.

Height: Tall enough
Sex: Male
Weapons: A bowl of soup, a serving spoon
Special Skills: Umm ... making soup
Favorite Colour: Brown
Weakness: Alcoholic
Intelligence: 1/10
Strength: 1/10
Speed: 1/10
Agility: 1/10
Fighting Skills: 1/10
Cooking Skills: 3/10
Catchphrase: It's time to cause a stir/ Here comes Soup-a-man

Crime fighting hat →

Big spoon →

'S' for Soup-a-man

→ Tomato soup

Boots for → tough terrain

Oru's Crew

Cap Kid
Powers:
1) Doesn't wear a top.
2) Always wears a hat.
3) Throws hats like ninja stars.
Weakness:
1) Throwing hats at someone doesn't stop them.

Gluten 3 Guy
Powers:
1) Endless supplies of gluten-free food.
2) Amazing cook.
3) Can eat nuts, and dairy products.
Weakness:
1) Alleric to gluten.
2) Gets a bad tummy easily.

Iron-Bru Man
Powers:
1) Ready to quench thirst.
Weakness:
1) Makes your teeth rot.

Stick Man!
Powers:
1) Throws sticks like no other.
Weakness:
1) Fire!!

Cap - Kid

IRON-BRU MAN

Gluten-3-Guy!

Stick MAN!

our manager Rachel

VISIBLE MAN ???

SNIDEY MAN

CAPTAIN CLICHE

LADY MAN

MAN~MAN

Ash's Fanspastic Five Superheroes

Snidey Man – Will make rude remarks behind your back.

Captain Cliché – He has every super-power a super-hero needs.

Lady Man – Draws upon the power of turning into a woman when needed.

Man Man – Drinks beer, lives and breathes football, whistles at women when they walk by. Weakness: Often pervs on Lady-Man ... then realises Lady-man is a man.

Visible Man – You can see Visible Man a mile off.

STEFAN'S GUIDE TO BEING IN BANDS

I think I'm what most people would call a Bandophile or a Band Pervert. I can't really remember off the top of my head how many bands I've been in but there's a saying that if you throw enough shit at the wall, some of it is bound to stick ... luckily, that sticky shit is The Midnight Beast.

Now let me teach you a little bit about how to run and maintain several bands at the same time in four easy steps ...

Step 1: Think of a good name

This applies to any of your bands. Don't choose a band name that's already been taken because then when they get more famous than you everyone will think you're just a tribute act. It happened to my old post-hardcore band, the Spice Girls ... such a shame. My previous band names include Ink, Killafornia, R.U.Twin, Icarus Burning, Stefan & The Artschool, Trick Fantastic, The Clik Clik, The Midnight Patrol, Perfect People, Chapters – and there's plenty more where they came from.

Hand on stomach

Step 2: Mix up your styles

There's no point being in three pop-punk bands, or eight death metal bands ... you'll never be able to tell the difference and you'll probably fuck up all the shows for your band mates. Why not have a Mexican hip/hop band, a booty-bass shakin' grindie band AND a Janet Jackson tribute act all at the same time?

Step 3: Do a ballbreaking photo shoot

By that I do not mean break your balls (if you have any) taking pictures, I just mean make it good ... so good that your (or your friends') balls break. Remember never to wear the same outfit in different shoots – most bands have a bit of style – even if it means dressing up in your mum's clothes. Here's some examples from some of my previous photo shoots ...

Stairs are cool

Step 4: Do NOT talk about your other band to your band

This will only lead to upset and cause hurt feelings. Nobody understands your need to succeed like you do ... Talking about your other band to your band will just confuse them into thinking you don't care about the music, which of course is the only reason you play in 26 bands DUMBASSSSSSSS!!!!!!! Oops, maybe make that 25.

And with that I bid you farewell on your quest to become the world's biggest band whore, so now go form some bands, you slut.

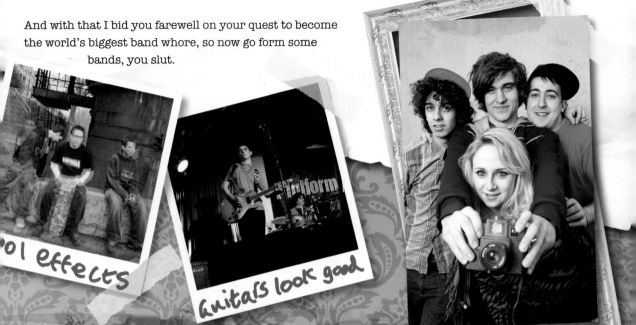

ol effects

Guitars look good

ASHLEY

Over the past few days I have been putting off writing the start of 'Ashley's section' in this book. I wanted it to open with a bang: I wanted it to be something witty or hilariously funny. I have realised it takes wit and humour to do that.

So maybe I could start with: 'Hi, I am Ashley. You may remember me from playing Ziggy in *EastEnders* or Lad in the *Doctor Who* Christmas Special.'

Or maybe I should let go of pretending to be a well-known actor among lots of London's pretty young things: 'Hi, I am Ashley. You may know me for being in The Midnight Beast.'

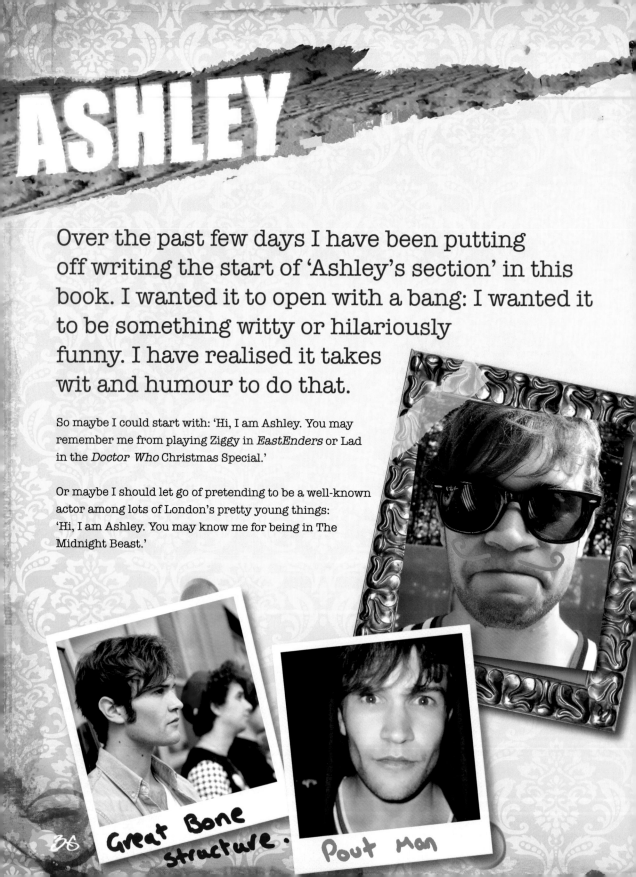

Great Bone Structure..

Pout Man

iDoL

That sounds a lot better.
And not so much up my own arse.

I entered this world on 4 January 1989.
This is an annoying date to be born. I get
two lots of presents very close together –
for Christmas and my birthday – and then
have to wait another 350-odd days until anyone
is generous to me again. How inconsiderate of my
parents. I was raised in Reading by Mama Horne
and Papa Horne. My early childhood years consisted
of running around my garden, pretending to be
Rambo, shooting objects with my gun finger and
having the fun ruined by my overly excited
dog Amber knocking me over, resulting in tears.
Rambo would have been disappointed
in me. A few years passed before my sister, Sarah-
Louise, joined the Horne dynasty. My parents said that when Sarah was born, she
brought me a present along with her. I had no idea how my mother had given birth to a
deluxe Playmobil fortress from Toys R Us ... but I was glad my sister
had made the effort all the same.

Football was a big part of my life. I liked
to play with balls. Even though I was
from Reading, I supported Newcastle
United because I liked the black and
white kit. Believe it or not, back then
they used to win games ... mental.
Strange as it may seem to you, I was quite
the skilled footballer: this retarded mover
was once playing semi-pro for Reading.
Through my time at school and my 'soccer
years', my mother blessed me with the most
trendy, girl-like haircut – the 90s boyband
favourite, 'The Curtains'. For those who do
not remember this travesty, it was a middle
parting with strands of hair either side,
framing the face. Just like this cheeky minx.
As I played football I could hear the other
boys' parents jest at me with lines like
'You go, girl,' and 'That girl's got skillz.'
They actually thought I was a girl. Lucky
boy/girl.

When I was 11 my poor grandad died. How? He fell asleep while having his cornflakes, dived head first into the bowl and drowned in the milk. Funny? I think NOT.

Another hobby of mine was acting. I bloody loved to act. At the young age of 12 I was faced with the dilemma: continue with my football or join a stage school for talented ballerinas and wannabe thespians with larger-than-life personalities? I chose the prestigious Sylvia Young Theatre School for Performing Arts. While I was there I got quite a few jobs through an agency. I was in musicals such as *Les Misérables*, *Doctor Dolittle*, *Chitty Chitty Bang Bang* and *Peter Pan*. You may also have heard my voice on many adverts. BOW DOWN to the Voiceover King. I am particularly proud of one voiceover: you know the geeky cartoon boy in the *Daily Express* adverts with the catchphrase, 'Express delivery'? That was me. Fuck yeah.

Throughout my time at Sylvia Young, my body structure and fashion sense changed quite dramatically:

Years 7/8

Small, lanky, long curtain hairstyle, freckles, market-stall skater clothes, e.g Wu-Tang Clan hoody, three-quarter-length denim shorts. DC shoes.

Year 9

In Year 9 I had started to become interested in girls (that's right, GIRLS ... not boys). I had also come to realise that the young ladies in my class only went wild for bad boys with street cred. I had to change.

Media Projects

Years 9/10

Still small, quite chubby and rounded, spiky hair, Bad Ass image, e.g. Nike pink polo shirt, Nike hoody, Kappa tracksuit bottoms and size 13 Timberland boots. Did this facade of top-of-the-range Nike gear work for me? Not in the slightest. Why did I have size 13 Timberland boots? Because I thought big shoes would make me look more domineering and manly. Instead it just made it very hard to walk and gave me a gammy leg.

Year 11

5'7", quiff hairstyle. Selection of unwanted Topman stock, e.g. black jacket with military buttons, white shirt, baggy jeans and patchwork grey shoes. Year 11 was also 'The Year of Ricky Gervais'. After becoming obsessed with *The Office* and watching it 24/7, I had picked up David Brent's personality and attributes. I basically became a middle-aged fat man from Slough. Any guy who didn't have a personality also became David Brent in any conversation. If – heaven forbid – you had two guys portraying Ricky Gervais in conversation, each guy would try and out-Brent the other, trying to fit in more of his catchphrases than his rival. I am sure everyone has a friend that resembles this paper merchant from Slough. In my final year photo, as sad as it may be, I am holding *The Office* box set as clear as day. Bloody hell. With this persona and my shoddy Topman garments I thought I was a ladykiller. Cool as fuck. I thought I was a stud, when really I was a ... DUD

Hot stuff

To further my education in the performing farts I joined the Italia Conti school. I didn't think five years of training in musical theatre were enough so I decided another three years would do the job. I had some bloody good times. Every day I would turn up for college, piss around with da boys Millen, Josh, Barke, Mack, Wayne, Jason and Sir Leon Garner. We'd do a few tap time steps, act out some Shakespeare and sing some bad-ass motherfucking musical tunes. At night we'd go out to a Wetherspoons pub, get wasted on ten pounds' worth of shots, head over to a karaoke bar, sing songs so out of tune it would make your ears bleed, get chased home by a crackhead drug dealer and finish the night off with a kebab. Living the dream. In that time I also got a few professional acting jobs. My first was a small part in Nickelodeon's hit show *Genie in the House*. I was part of a fake boyband who sang hit songs about pineapples and shit. Not one

DA-BOYZ

of the best moments of my career. Next I got the part of Ziggy in *EastEnders*. I was part of a chavvy crew 'E17' who bullied old women, and stabbed young boys. If I remember correctly I am sure the director said, 'If you lads do well, the writers will give you more storylines.' As it turns out, my storyline got the most complaints ever on *EastEnders* at the time. Oh crap, that was the end of that. My last job was playing the part of Lad in the *Doctor Who* Christmas Special 2008. I had one golden line: 'Who the hell is that?' and I still get fan mail to this very day. One avid fan wrote: 'I like the way you played the part of Lad.' Why thank you, sir, it was a tough role to play and I have no clue why I wasn't nominated for a BAFTA.

From actor to just another Boyband

This adventure of mine started early December, when I was awoken from my drunken slumber by a very excitable Stefan Abingdon and Dru Francis Wakely. They seemed to have forgotten we had all gone out the night before on a drunken rampage of stealing drinks and consuming them as quickly as we could. Stefan and Dru had come up with a new song. They seemed to come up with songs like it was going out of fashion. But this song was different, it was a PARODY! Stef explained it was Ke$ha's number one hit 'Tik Tok'. The lyrics were 'bloody fucking nuts', and they decided to make a home-made video to go alongside the track. Dr Dru asked if I would like to participate in the video but I was not willing to let go of my respected acting career and join in with the antics. While Stefan and Dru would take centre stage of this parody, I would let the dancer in me parade around in the background showing off my retro – yet modern – style of dance.

That night Stefan Abadingdong edited the footage we had caught on our very basic video camera. On 13 December 2009 'Tik Tok' was uploaded to YouTube. Now what do I do? I had never put anything on the World Wide Web before. All I knew is that it was a very dangerous place where the most powerful of men could be struck down and mocked by the opinions of young kids who wanted their points to be heard. I posted our little video on Facebook. If any of my friends wanted to check me out acting like a mental they could. Throughout the day I checked how the video was doing. After an hour we had 301 views and as many comments. Our friends were actually watching us piss around in Stefan's house. They clearly had too much time on their hands. After two hours we had over 2000 views. By now I thought my friends definitely had too much time on their hands. After eight hours: 8000 views. I worked out that's 1000 views an hour – I am pretty famous among my friends for my maths skills. From looking at the comments I also worked out it wasn't just my friends who were watching, it was also random YouTubers. How did they discover our masterpiece? By the evening we had over 10,000 views. I could now go to bed a happy man.

The Big Apple

Stefan Abingdon

We first met at an audition for a kids' nursery rhyme video way back in 1998. He was a cool young chappy with a mini 'fro. I was a lanky nerd with curtains. The curtain hairstyle was hip in 1998. FACT.

For the audition we had to improvise dance moves. Stefan's was a bad-ass breakdance and he busted some moves I could only dream of pulling off. I was next, what could I do?
A few turns maybe? Should I attempt a backflip? Instead I merged together a few star jumps while punching the air in an angry way. Did this get me and the 'fro the job? Of course it did. We were born to dance.

I have been sleeping on Stefan's floor ever since.

France

COCK.

NO PARKING
ON THIS PAVEMENT

New School

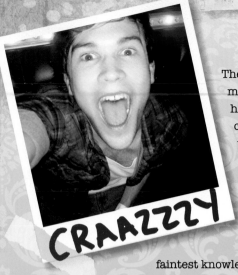

CRAAZZZY

The next morning I woke up, had a morning wee, made salmon and cream cheese on toast, had a shower and then logged on to my computer. I checked to see how the video was doing. It had a casual 25,000 views ... TWENTY-FIVE THOUSAND VIEWS?! I rang up Stefan. He told me that Perez Hilton and Ke$ha herself had tweeted out our video to their fan base. I hadn't the faintest knowledge of what 'tweeted out' meant but I was grateful all the same. The comments on our creation were coming in every few seconds. 'They are so fit', 'This is better than Ke$ha's', 'The guy in the back looks like Stifler'. I look like Stifler? Do you mean the womaniser in *American Pie* who seems to make a tit out of himself in most situations? It wasn't just Stifler people thought I looked like; Chace Crawford was another that came up quite a lot, too. A guy in *Gossip Girl* who does more pouting than acting? Secretly I was happy with either of them.

CREW

By the end of the week the parody had over 250,000 views. That's 250,000 more views than I thought it would ever get. Viewers were commenting as if The Midnight Beast was an actual band. Had I suddenly made the transition from being a wannabe thespian to ROCK STAR?! I had always gone to gigs where Stefan and Dru would showcase their latest band: Icarus Burning, Perfect People, Ink, The Clik Clik, to name just a few. I think I must have been their number one groupie but now I was part of the gang, no longer a fangirl. OH YEAHHHH.

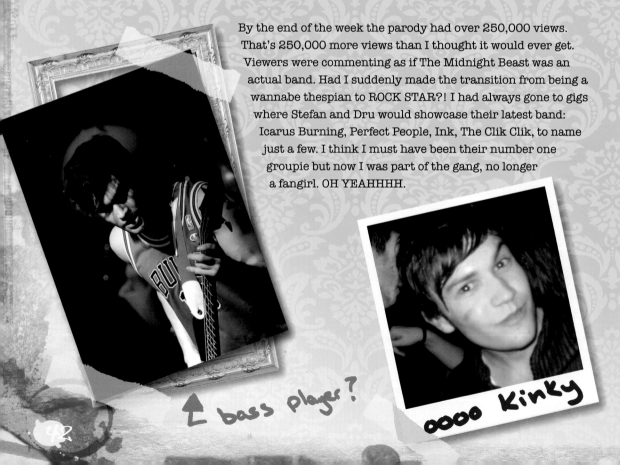

⬅ bass player?

oooo Kinky

Dru Wakely

I first came across Dru in the summer of 2002 ... or 2003 ... or 2004. Believe it or not, there was not a hair to be seen upon his smooth and youthful face. He was in a band named Icarus Burning, they played classics such as 'Jezebel', 'Achalasia', 'Did You Wrong' and 'My Summer'. Mr Wakely liked to drum, so in order to be friends with him I created the lie that I also liked to drum. I once met him in Putney to get a pair of drumsticks I would never use. I even bought a drum kit and sold it within a month. To this day I still pretend I can drum. Dru still believes me. Suckerrrrrr.

beadles

SNUG

It was Christmas Day 2009. I had found out that year that Santa wasn't real. There was no Christmas spirit left in my body. I moped downstairs, opened the presents 'Mr Claus' had got me and then logged on to the web. Surely nothing could cheer me up, or could it? I had forced myself to start a Twitter account; now people would know what pointless events made up my day. As soon as I logged into twatter, I was bombarded with messages: 'The Midnight Beast are on the front page of MTV.com.' My small girly fingers typed in the website as quickly as they could and to my surprise TMB *were* on the front page of MTV.com ... HELL YEAH!! Christmas was back on!

The Midnight Beast in the future

It's the year 2013 and I am part of a failed musical comedy trio. The *Guardian* gave TMB's E4 series 0 stars out of 10 and *Heat* gave it 10 lipsticks out of 10. This is very bad news indeed. This year you will find me making a desperate attempt at fame by appearing on such hit shows as *I'm a Celebrity* (Z-lebrity), *Big Brother Austria*, *The Only Way is Putney* and *Justin Lee Collins Brings Back The Midnight Beast*. You might also find me making personal appearances at children's birthday parties, dressed as a clown, making balloon animals ...

lez be friends

LESBIAN

GIRL MACHINE

18

Nick Hoult~
Hoult~ Famous
Good Friend

44

RIDER
DEMANDS

Touring can be fun, but being away from our home comforts is not. Here are some of our more demanding requests when it comes to picking the perfect backstage rider.

The Midnight Beast
Rider

x3 Waters
x3 Towels
x2 X-Large Condoms
x1 X-Small Condom
x3 Doughnuts (with middle taken out!!)
x3 Juggling Midgets (never above 3ft)
Assorted Nuts
Chewing gum
Crisps + Dip
7 bottles of russian vodka (non-Alcoholic)
x1 Audi TT
NO eye contact!

And a cab note home! :)

DRU'S GUIDE TO COMEBACKS

'Take that, bitch!'

Here are some blunt, to the point and downright rude comebacks that I use frequently.

'I'm having a conversation, A, B, C-yourself out'

This is a great one if someone is trying to butt into a conversation you're already having with another person. As you say it, simply point to yourself as A, then to the person you are talking to as B and the person butting in as C before quickly pointing to the door to tell them where to go.

'Your mum'

Standard one-liner that is great to use if someone has just insulted you. For example, if someone says to you: 'Your hair looks like Hitler's,' you can simply reply 'Your mum's hair looks like Hitler's!' or if they say 'Your beard looks well gay,' your comeback should be simple: 'Your mum's beard looks well gay!' This will usually kill off any threat of another comeback but just watch out for a fist – people can be twitchy when it comes to mothers.

'And what?!'

Translation: 'Can I help you, sir?' This can be used in any context. My favourite point to use it is when I catch someone looking at me. A simple raise of the shoulders and a stern 'AND WHAT?' should get them to cower away in fear.

'You fucking what?!'

This is just a slightly more aggressive version of the above. Best used when you're feeling more irate.

44

'Fuck are you looking at?'

Tired of having somebody stare at you on the tube or something?
Caught someone repeatedly turning round to watch you or see what you're
doing? Then give them a blunt, angry 'Fuck are you looking at?' You can use this
one to different degrees. You might find muttering it under your breath so it is just
audible does the trick or you may prefer to say it really loud so lots of people can hear
to get that mass effect.

'Are you having a fucking laugh?'

This comeback is most effective when somebody has presented you with a bold statement like,
'I'll slap you in a minute' or 'You should run to the shop and get us a drink.' Using 'Are you
having a fucking laugh?' quickly shows how outraged you are at the thought of what that
person has said.

'Fuck off!'

Possibly the best comeback ever and a personal favourite of mine. You could try it out in
different ways:

'Fuuuuuuuck off!' – slightly prolong the fuck to show a light-hearted tone.
'Fuck OFF!' – really emphasise the word 'off' to show you've really had enough.
And when all else fails, try a quick, loud, blunt and straight to the point 'FUCK OFF!'

Let me demonstrate how effective it can be:
Ash: 'Swearing is bad, Dru.'
Dru: 'Fuck off!'
Job done.

Now that's about all the comeback phrases I'm going to share with you.
After all, I can't be giving all my best lines away. But fear not as I will
leave you with a few more insults to help you out in
your time of need ... Enjoy!

* You fucking bellend
* Twat
* knob jockey
* Dickhead
* Piss off, prick
* Arsewipe
* Sperm-in-a-tor

PLAYING WITH HADOUKEN AT KOKO

by Ash

It was another dull afternoon. Me, Stefan and Dru were walking back home from Putney Leisure Centre. We would go to the gym in a group because we were afraid of the bigger boys at the weights – you know, the ones who make needless loud noises and poop their pants while lifting 50kg. Scary *shiiit*! After a sweaty session of a few sit-ups, a light jog and some star jumps, we would finish off by heading over to the local pub or kebab house for a healthy luncheon.

Our topic of conversation was 'Who has the hairiest body?' – gripping stuff – when we received a call from Nick Rice, the drummer of Hadouken!, an indie/grime/electronica outfit. He wondered if The Midnight Beast might want to play a tiny set to open their show at KOKO. We were flattered and the only problem was TMB had never played a gig before. Stef and Dru had bucketloads of experience in their previous bands, Ink, Icarus Burning, Killafornia, R.U.Twin, The Clik Clik, Perfect People, Chapters ... (the list goes on and on). I, on the other hand, only had experience in jumping around my room to Limp Bizkit. We took up the offer: 'twas time to start bringing our YouTube videos to the stage.

Rehearsals were a time for playing 'Would you rather?', doing retarded walks, animal noises and farts, crude jokes and eating pizza; and this took priority over practising our set for KOKO. Good job, guys.

Suddenly it was the day of the show and all we had gained from rehearsals was weight from the snacks. Our gear consisted of 1 x ironing board (for our DJ), 1 x makeshift Midnight Beast sign, 3 x foam swords and 3 x red jackets. We spare no expense. Our rider consisted of a few bottles of water, some fruit and beer stolen from the Hadouken! dressing room – we were ninjas after all. Being our first set, we honestly thought no one would have heard of us, that we'd get the weirdest looks and most likely be booed off stage. The lights went off, our TMB sign shone like a beacon of hope, 'Lez-Be-Friends' kicked in and we clumsily staggered on stage. The crowd went INSANE. The set started and straight away my mic lead fell out. I couldn't find it and panic set in. Why did this have to happen to me? Dru saw it and passed it to Stef; Stef passed it to me and as cool as you like I slipped it back in. Now that's what I call teamwork, ya'll. We bounced around the stage like three Duracell bunnies playing 'Lez-Be-Friends', 'Ninjas' and 'Tik Tok', and we left everybody wanting more. HIGH FIVE, TEAM ASHDRUSTEF!

MINESWEEPING

'Ninjas of the Dancefloor' did not write itself, it was all inspired by a little game called 'Minesweeping' – and here's the rules...

This is a very easy game to play. It requires a lack of morals and it's very important that you have no self-respect. It is pretty much just played by students – or broke musicians.

The first thing you will need to do is gain entry to a nightclub, preferably one with a VIP area (make sure you don't pay to get in). The next step is to check your surroundings and plan your getaway. Now remind yourself this is not theft, it's a game of taking advantage of your surroundings. Spot a drink that has been poured from a bottle of the complimentary spirit and left on its own, grab it, make a quick dash and consume responsibly.

The hat-trick: time it so that a barman is just about to pour away a pre-made drink, walk up to it and deliver the line, 'I'm sorry, sir, this drink is mine.' You will no doubt feel a small sense of pride, until you realise you're a thieving little toerag.

WORKING WITH THE BBC ON HOUSE PARTY

By now we'd started getting emails from various 'big shot' managers, agents, promoters and production companies, but one name we couldn't ignore was the BBC.

It's the B-B-FUCKING-C, the only channel installed on your TV whether you want it or not ... pretty big time for three little dirty-mouthed nobodies. They wanted to make a video with us and we wanted to do anything they said, so naturally we went in for a chat. I am not used to being told what to do and not very good at handling it either so luckily we were met with a comfortable, 'You can do whatever you want, as long as it's topical.' Topical is not really a word that means much to The Midnight Beast. Sure, we joke about the current number one and who's just come out on the front page of the *Sun*, but topical usually means stuff to do with the news ... and my God, we NEVER watch the news (embarrassing as it is to say).

We decided against doing a football song for the World Cup since I know nothing about football – much to the other guys' amusement – and instead we picked the election. We knew even less about that. I'm not quite sure how we ended up with eight lubed-up teenagers dancing around half-naked in a BBC office, but it happened and we'll never forget it ...

cheddar

double fringe

TMB PARTY

We ran for election in 2010 and although we triumphed,
we were booted out two days afterwards because of the following policies.

The TMB Party will:

Make all pavements from bouncy castle material to add a spring to your step. This will decrease travel times.

Ban traffic lights – drive wherever you want, whenever you want. This will prevent road rage.

Change the police uniform from blue to pink to make people feel less threatened.

Make-up shall be banned – we will see the true form of the woman. This will decrease birth rates.

Citizens will be legally compelled to learn a fact about the person sitting to their right on public transport: this will make the world a friendlier place.

Everybody is required to have their own theme tune. This will encourage character-building and increase confidence.

All chat-up lines are banned; they suck.

Every form of education must have a milk-and-nap time; this will encourage bone growth and brain development.

All tap water shall be replaced with energy drinks; this will improve performance of the body and mind.

The dress code smart/casual shall not exist, it is silly and pointless and nobody understands it.

ASK STEF

Dear Stefan,
All of my so-called friends at school take the mickey out of me because I've got curly hair. They call me names like 'Curly Fries', 'Curly-Curly-Fish Face', 'Scarecrow Head' and other names that really hurt my feelings. You look like someone who's been called every name under the sun, so how can I make them stop?
Liam, Godstone

Well first of all, thanks. I didn't choose this hair. When I was younger I used to cut it all off, but unfortunately the only reason curly-haired people have curly hair is because underneath they've got an abnormally small, misshapen head ... so the names only got worse without it, as you might imagine. The best thing to do is start convincing your classmates that curly-haired people are cool. You could say, 'Hey guys, have you heard Mika?' OK, sorry, maybe that's a bit far-fetched. Instead, how about, 'Do you guys watch *Misfits*? Robert Sheehan is sex on legs!' This will lead them into a false sense of security so they start trusting you as a human being rather than thinking you are a circus freak. Good luck, Curly Fries!

Dear Stefan,
I was recently arrested for indecent exposure in a tree outside my uncle's house. It's been in the paper with my picture and nobody believes that I was just trying out my new binoculars and I had forgotten to put any clothes on. Please help. I've lost all my friends.

Dean, Essex

Hang in there, Dean, we've all been there. Who hasn't had a cheeky peek at their neighbour's privates on a rainy day? You have to admit you're guilty, though: your alibi sucks and nobody forgets to get dressed. You're a pervert, a nudist AND a peeping Tom and you desperately need help. Call a psychologist, sicko.

DRU TALKS ABOUT INVASION DAY AT BRIGHTON BEACH

So The Midnight Beast were summoned, for some reason, to play only their second ever live show at the infamous Great Escape Festival in May 2010. Now, this was not at any of the usual music venues that Brighton has to offer (probably because they were sick of seeing my and Stefan's faces yet again after we'd played them all in various other bands). No, our venue this time was on a pier with a big green doughnut on it. Not a real doughnut; that would be silly. Plus they're not usually green. Unless they've gone off.

Anyway, we turned up at Brighton beach to find a small stage, big enough to fit two singers on with a sound system that could just about cope with an acoustic act. On the plus side it was a stage that was sponsored by an energy drink so I got a sticker, a key ring and a free can of energy. Words cannot describe my happiness at that moment in time.

Cheeky

Dru has t

The madness began when we made our way, gear in arms, to the stage. Yeah, that's right – this was before we had roadies who carried all our equipment and a tour crew to wait on us hand and foot. We started to notice that we were being followed by a few groups of people and before long more and more started to come up to us asking for pictures and autographs. It was crazy considering we felt like we had jumped straight off the Internet on to a stage where we pranced around and sang about lesbians. Pretty appropriate in a town known for being the gay capital of England.

Loving it

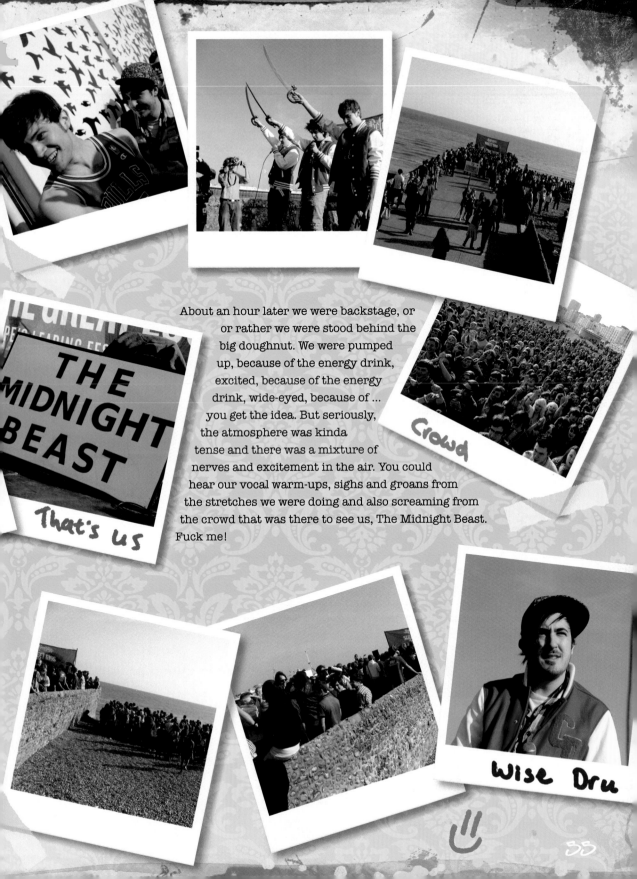

About an hour later we were backstage, or
or rather we were stood behind the
big doughnut. We were pumped
up, because of the energy drink,
excited, because of the energy
drink, wide-eyed, because of ...
you get the idea. But seriously,
the atmosphere was kinda
tense and there was a mixture of
nerves and excitement in the air. You could
hear our vocal warm-ups, sighs and groans from
the stretches we were doing and also screaming from
the crowd that was there to see us, The Midnight Beast.
Fuck me!

THE
MIDNIGHT
BEAST

That's us

Crowd

Wise Dru

There is no way I can write how shocked and surprised we were at the turnout to that particular show. I mean, we were expecting a good 70 or 80 people, and I honestly mean that. But look! So when we looked out at the pier and saw we had a human barrier at the front of the stage with screaming excited people all the way up the pier, spilling out on to the street, we were pretty taken aback to say the least. I think I heard someone say we shut down the Great Escape Festival for the 15–20 minutes we were on, which isn't bad for a comedy trio in their twenties who laugh at toilet humour.

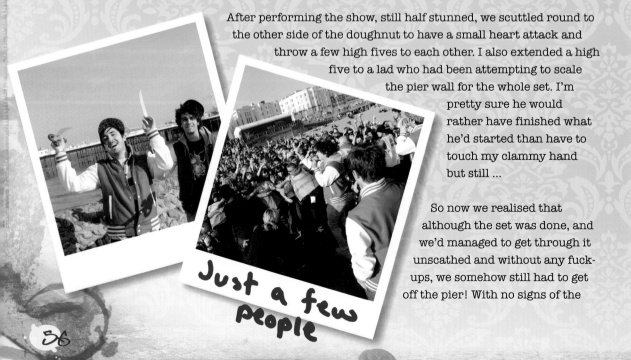

After performing the show, still half stunned, we scuttled round to the other side of the doughnut to have a small heart attack and throw a few high fives to each other. I also extended a high five to a lad who had been attempting to scale the pier wall for the whole set. I'm pretty sure he would rather have finished what he'd started than have to touch my clammy hand but still …

So now we realised that although the set was done, and we'd managed to get through it unscathed and without any fuck-ups, we somehow still had to get off the pier! With no signs of the

Just a few people

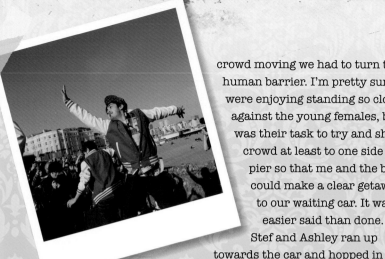

crowd moving we had to turn to our human barrier. I'm pretty sure they were enjoying standing so close up against the young females, but it was their task to try and shift the crowd at least to one side of the pier so that me and the boys could make a clear getaway to our waiting car. It was easier said than done. Stef and Ashley ran up towards the car and hopped in no problems. I, on the other hand, got stuck behind a security man who thought I was one of the crowd – an easy mistake to make, I'm sure. After hitting him repeatedly, he clocked what had happened and threw me in the car. With everyone finally aboard we managed to drive away, but not before having the car rocked about like we were some sort of pop stars. Anyone would have thought Bieber or the Beatles were in the back, not us three.

ANGER Problems

As the car drove off, it headed down some of Brighton's side streets, and a small crowd continued to chase us. Within this group, there was a boy with his arm in a sling, but hats off to him, he still ran as fast as he could. In fact, he ran so much that he tripped over his own shoes and as he did his trousers came down. Most people would know when enough is enough but this dude carried on. So my friend, if you're reading this – and you'll know who you are – this book is dedicated to you. (Well from me it is anyway. I haven't cleared that with anyone officially yet, but fuck it.) I only dedicate it to him on the condition that he is actually a fan and didn't instead think the car contained Jedward or somebody!

So Brighton, we salute you for your human barrier; for your kid in a sling tripping over his own feet and causing his trousers to fall down; for your big green doughnut; and for not taking offence to a lesbian song. We love you!

50 THINGS
THE MIDNIGHT BEAST HATE

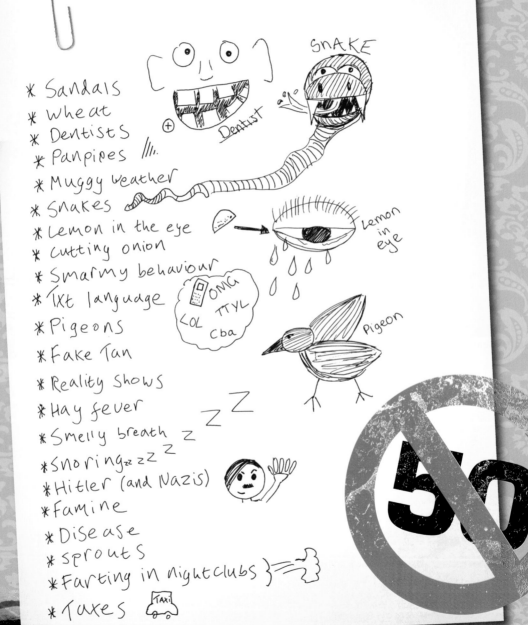

* Sandals
* Wheat
* Dentists
* Panpipes
* Muggy weather
* Snakes
* Lemon in the eye
* Cutting onion
* Smarmy behaviour
* Txt language
* Pigeons
* Fake Tan
* Reality shows
* Hay fever
* Smelly breath
* Snoring
* Hitler (and Nazis)
* Famine
* Disease
* Sprouts
* Farting in nightclubs
* Taxes

Dentist

SnAKE

Lemon in eye

OMG TTYL LOL Cba

Pigeon

* Wasps (and bees) *bzzz*
* Paper cuts
* Pepple beaches
* Ball in the face
* Getting Windled
* Irish twin popstars
* mediocre teen soap operas
* Dumbo plug ears
* Loud people on buses
* Personal space invasion
* Playing music from mobiles
* Namedroppers
* Flares
* Men who wear thongs as beachwear
* Fog
* Astro turf
* Grazed knees
* Touching suede
* Scraping nails on a blackboard
* Knife and fork squeak

* Noisy eaters
* Racists
* Boybands
* Boy racers
* Fox noises
* Charity muggers
* Sex in public
* Parodies

Now Playing

squeaaak!

man
thong
sand

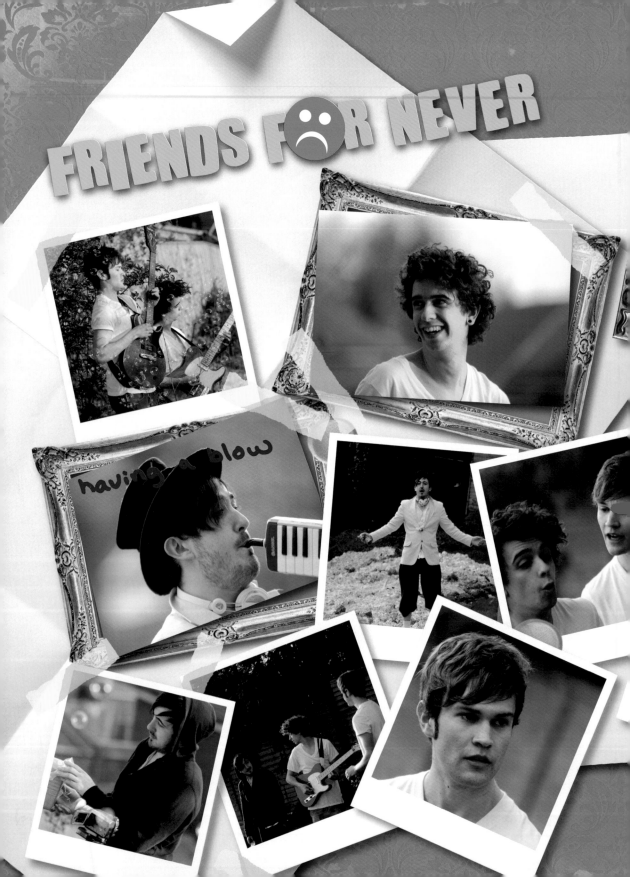

THE MIDNIGHT BEAST

Sepia Friends

~~freak~~ voice weak

e!!

Lock your babies up!

61

Agony Aunt

ASK DRU

Dear Dru,
I recently came home from a night out with some friends and, drunk as a skunk, I decided to pleasure myself in the comfort of my own room. Unfortunately I fell asleep with *ahem* cock in hand, and I awoke to find someone had been in my room and placed a blanket over my naked self. I think it was my dad. What do I do?
Mathew

Hey there, Mathew. Well that is quite a predicament to say the least. I'm afraid if you've been caught there is no going back. You can do one of three things. You can embrace the fact that your father has seen what all men have and just act normally with him – maybe whisper 'thank you' in his ear. Your second option is you could try and lie your way out of it and claim that you were checking for things that shouldn't be there. *Or* you can try and find out if it even was him that came in. Watch out for his eye contact and if things seem weird, it definitely was him. Hope that helps!

Dear Dru,
I was walking down my local high street when I spotted a homeless man. I was in a generous mood and went to put down a fiver when I accidentally put a note down with my number on which I was supposed to give to this girl I like. Now it's two weeks on and the homeless guy hasn't stopped calling me and just the other night I had a voicemail that was just heavy breathing. Today he even asked me out. HELP!
Steve Wallace

Wow, Steve, you're fucked!
All the best, Dru.

Dear Dru,
A girl at my school recently offered me some Calpol. She said it was a really cool, chilled drug that everyone is taking. I didn't take it and now she's started to call me names and other people also join in. I'm so tempted, what should I do?
Alice Titfield

Hello Alice,
Well let me tell you from first-hand experience that drugs are not the way. Especially Calpol. Shit, look how I turned out. With a name like Titfield, I'm sure the kids at school will soon find something else to bully you over; so don't worry, the drug phase should soon pass. Remember my school motto: If in doubt, give a teacher a shout! Dru

DADDY

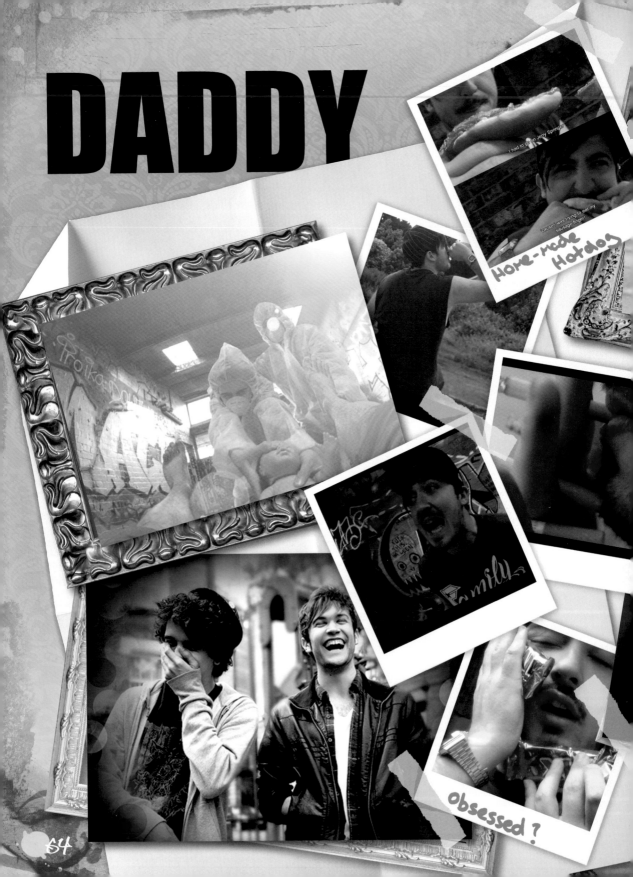

I had to go on Jerry Springer

'cause I was trying to eat my sausage finger!

Home-made Hotdog

obsessed?

LOVEBOX, SKYFEST AND LATITUDE

by Stefa...

FRIDAY 16TH JULY

DIZZEE RASCAL

CHASE & STATUS

NOISETTES
ELLIE GOULDING
THE MIDNIGHT BEAST
NEWHAM GENERALS | SMURFIE SYCO

NYC DOWNLOW
ZINC & DYNAMITE MC
MISTAJAM RADIO 1
JOY ORBISON
MJ COLE || URCHINS

MORE STAGES

THE **MACCABEES**
MYSTERY JETS
BOMBAY BICYCLE CLUB
CHEW LIPS || TINASHE
MAVERICK SABRE

FAVELA CHIC BIG TOP
XFM SOUNDSYSTEM
GAYMERS BANDSTAND
CUERVO STREET FIESTA
PLUS MORE TBA

DANCE STAGE
RELENTLESS ENERGY DRINK
CROOKERS || BRODINSKI
SINDEN || RIVA STARR || DOORLY

RIZLA ARENA
TODD EDWARDS
TODDLA T & MC SEROCEE
ZOMBIE DISCO SQUAD
STICKY & THE HEATWAVE || COOLY G

VIP AREA WITH KITSUNE MAISON FEATURING
JAYMO & ANDY GEORGE (RADIO 1), LATE OF THE PIER (DJ SET)
PUNKS JUMP UP • IS TROPICAL - PLAY PAUL - LUCA C
JBAG (JERRY BOUTHIER & ANDREA GORGERINO)

Last summer was our first summer on the festival circuit, so not wanting to do things by halves, we decided to cram three into one hectic weekend ...

Lovebox was our first festival ever and we were playing it with Dizzee Rascal. I once met Dizzee in a haunted house in Jonathan Ross's garden. I was dressed as Batman's sidekick, Robin. Dizzee was scared and hid behind me the whole way round (not many people can tell such a story without starting it with the words, 'I had this odd dream last night,' but it really happened to me). Anyway we were excited and nervous about kicking off our festival career, and luckily lots of die-hard fans turned up to cheer us on. We even got given some free watches and I'd like to believe this was Lovebox's way of saying they'd had the time of their lives.

Next up, we played Skyfest for Sky TV which was pretty RAD. Our dressing room was next to Jordan's and we nearly got in trouble when she tried to eat our best friend's poisonous frog (again, another story that sounds like a dream but I can assure you is totally real). Jordan performed her single and was booed off stage. We had to follow that but the audience seemed to lap up our whole set, especially 'Just Another Boyband' (I reckon we should've changed it to 'Just Another Big-Boobs' for that day, though). Also big props to Sky for giving us 100 food tokens. I don't think any of us will eat again.

Dizze

hell
yo

Last but not least it was
Latitude who supplied us with
enough alcohol to tranquilise a
small country. We took on the
challenge of drinking it all and ended
up dancing to reggae at 4 a.m. We had a nice,
early, hungover set. We thought nobody would come
but boy did they flood in. We were playing on a tiny, tiny stage in a tent made for comedians. Our
fans bolted to the front, kicking over all the picnic hampers and glasses of wine left by the fleeing
audience from
the previous calm performance, and we proceeded to blitz through a life-changing set where our
DJ decided to drop 'Tik Tok' twice.

Over the course of these days we managed to invent a new game
called 'WOBBLE YOUR FACE AROUND SO
THAT THE CAMERA PICKS OUT A STUPID
EXPRESSION'.

Here are the results ...

WORSERY RHYMES

Hey diddle, diddle,
The penguin was fiddled,
By the doggy that lived down the road.
A hitman was hired,
And two shots were fired,
Now the doggy won't fiddle again.

Twinkle, twinkle, little star,
One day you'll go really far,
Into bed with lots of men,
Promising you'll work for them.
Twinkle, twinkle, little star,
Holly wood knows where you are.

Humpty Dumpty sat on the wall,
Humpty Dumpty's too fat and small,
Jamie Oliver's school dinner rules,
Couldn't save Humpty from a heart attack.

Three blind mice, three blind mice,
See how they run, see how they run.
They smelt cheese across the motorway,
They ran but couldn't look either way,
Did you ever see so ~~mg~~ much blood in your life
From three dead mice
Three.
Dead.
Mice.

A VISIT TO SEE MR TOM DEACON

It was Sunday 1 August and The Midnight Beast did their first radio interview at BBC Radio 1 ... live! We were all pretty damn excited about taking a li'l trip to see the legend that is Mr Tom Deacon, to chat about our first single, 'Booty Call'. We started off at Stefan's house, giggling away like little kids high on sugar and trying our hardest not to swear so that we got used to the idea in time to go on national radio. As you can imagine, I found this task particularly difficult and needless to say it didn't last long. In fact I think we were all swearing right up until we sat down with Tom – good start!

Dressed in the same jeans (*cooool*!), we headed to a nearby shop to pick up some Red Bull to aid us in being mental – and funny. We got novelty-size cans – as Stef calls them: you know, the needlessly large ones that would probably kill you if you had a very weak heart – and on the way the silly antics began when Stef found a giant cone to shout through. As Ash said, he sounded like a distressed whale. Ash got it into his head that we were walking all the way to Radio 1. Silly boy.

YEAH!

So with cans in our hands, and black skinny jeans on our legs we proceeded – by car – to head into central London for our interview. When we arrived we were completely shocked and overwhelmed to find a huge crowd outside. But we quickly saw sense and realised that The Wanted were already inside and the fans were mainly there for them. To our surprise, though, as we walked round the corner to get in we were met by a rush of people who had come to see us! We felt flattered and very excited as they began chanting 'Midnight Beast! Midnight Beast!' as we headed downstairs into the depths of the Radio 1 building. I had a wee in the girls' toilets and Stefan had a long Red Bull wee and then suddenly it was chatty time with Tom. We were live and we could not swear. *Shiiiiiiiit!*

After filling everyone in on what we'd been up to, Tom decided to make Ash play a game where he had to fit as many chocolates in his mouth as possible within a time limit. Ash tried ... but failed. Afterwards he felt pretty poorly. With all the banter over, it was music time. Our first single was introduced and it was definitely a weird yet amazing feeling having your track played on Radio 1. We said our goodbyes to our newly made friend and promised we'd be back very soon with a new song.

Thanks Tom and the crew and Radio 1!

4th member

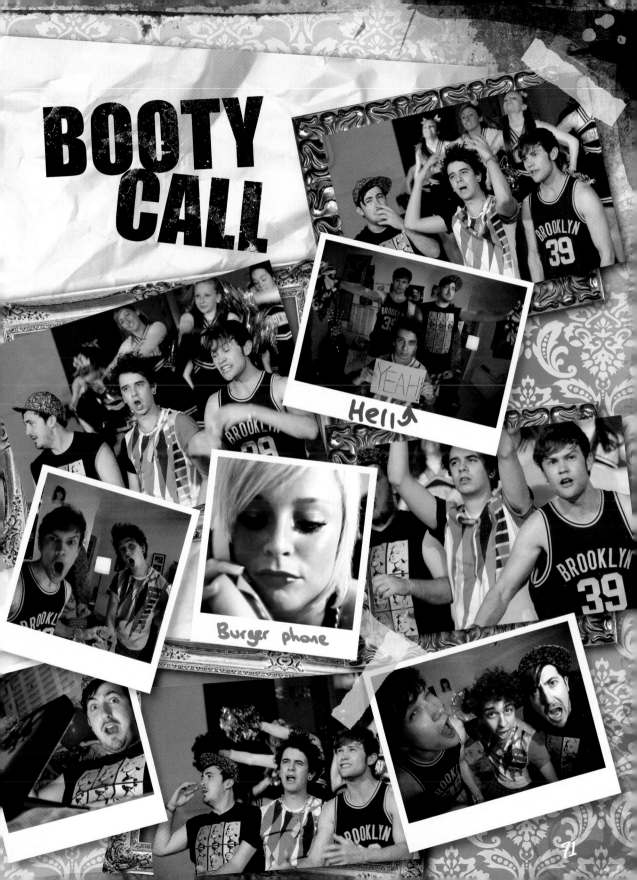

BOOTY CALL

Hello

YEAH!

Burger phone

READING AND LEEDS FESTIVAL 2010 – ASH

Summer had come around once again – the birds were chirping, the sun was shining and my small village of Caversham was filled with the sounds of festival-goers. When Reading fest arrives, Caversham sees the most action it gets all year round – Waitrose is a cattle market as people rush in for supplies (alcohol/condoms/toilet roll: all the essentials); 'the unwashed' queue around the block for a quick clean in Costa Coffee's toilet and Warings Bakery hires in heavy security to stop crazy individuals from stealing their outside table-and-chair sets. The year 2010 was different, though – the big joke known as The Midnight Beast had been asked to play at this notorious event. Every year I would listen to Reading's headline act from across the river in the comfort of my back garden; this year I would actually be playing on one of the stages. Was I nervous? Fuck no. Well, maybe a little …

Playing mid-afternoon on the Alternative Stage, we didn't really expect much of a crowd. We were up against a lot of established bands who had been together for years and me, Stefan and Dru had barely joined forces for five minutes so far.

But ten minutes before we were due to play, I could already hear voices chanting 'MIDNIGHT BEAST!' from inside the tent. Did this mean people had actually come to see us, three nobodies who pretended to bum each other on stage to music? I crept to the side of the tent to see if we had drawn a crowd. All I could see was a rammed front few rows. Some girls caught a glimpse of me and screamed. I was just as scared as they seemed to be, so I ran back to the dressing room to report my findings.

Nothing could have prepared me and the boys for the sight we were about to witness when we stepped out on stage. The 5000 capacity tent was packed, and bursting out of all entrances were people who were ready to PARTAYY with the Beast. We may have already had millions of views on our videos, but we knew that didn't mean we were guaranteed a crowd as big as this. The next 25 minutes were MENTAL. We danced our little socks off while the crowd of thousands jumped around, singing along to all our songs.

Sadly, our small set had come to an end. We played 'Tik Tok', the crowd went WILD, and we walked off stage with big smiles across our cheeky little faces. The moment we had left the tent, the chants of 'ENCORE' were booming out. Holy cow, Batman, we had nothing prepared for an encore! It was time to bust out 'House Party', and to the lyrics, 'David Cam can't do the running man,' and 'Gordon Brown can't break it down,' a mosh pit was created. That's how we roll.

As we came off stage we were buzzing but there was no time to rest. We had to make a mad rush over to the NME tent for a few interviews, then into the festival area to meet with fans. We three Beasts ran from one side of the site to the other, stopping for photos and autographs on the way. When we were done, Stef and Dru jumped into the tour van and I followed up the rear (ooh, kinky) in my car with Showbiz Simon and we went hell for leather up to Leeds. Showbiz Simon is a dear friend to us all. He casually struts around with TMB, or the political movement known as the Green Party, in his sparkly gold jacket for all to admire.

We arrived in Leeds just after 10 p.m and it was wet, dark and muddy. I had never camped before and this wasn't exactly a pleasant first experience. Setting up a tent in the pitch black while getting drenched is quite messy and mud splashed everywhere: Dirty Ashley. We had a few drinks and then it was time to get into my makeshift abode. With my head on my pillow (bag), I nodded off to the sound of a very horny couple in the next tent having incredibly LOUD sexual intercourse. How *loverly*. The following morning I woke up, went for an urgent piss, found a few used condoms in my path and strolled over for a much needed shower. My gonads were so small and shrivelled you might have mistaken me for a little wee girl.

Like the night before, we still didn't expect to have a huge audience but we were stunned once more by the thousands of cool cats flocking to the Alternative Stage to see TMB. The set was just as crazy as Reading, encore and all. We were welcomed with champagne in our trailer from the generous big cheeses at Festival Republic but I was a tiny bit disappointed that they hadn't hired us a few dirty hookers. Then again, nobody likes an STD.

Strange as it may seem, we were asked to replace the mighty Guns N' Roses as the headline act that evening. We sadly declined, knowing the most likely outcome would be a trip to A&E for me, Dru and Stef after getting submerged in bottles of piss. To this day I am not sure if the offer was real or a joke ... either way, I was flattered. The following summer we were invited back as the headline act on the Festival Republic stage. Not bad for three idiots. Hell to the mother-fucking yeah.

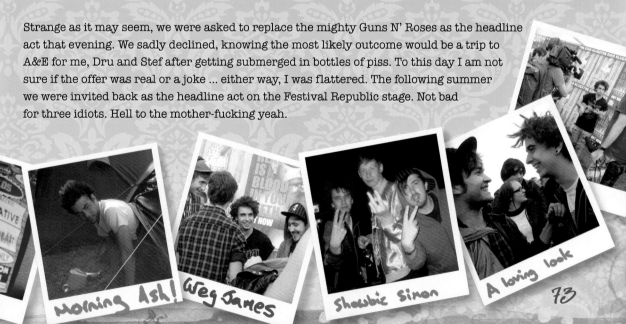

They really smelled

Morning Ash!   Wey James   Showbiz Simon   A loving look

HoW To SuRVIVE A ZOMBIE APOCALYPSE

So it's 2016 and we survived 2012 without an ice age or the sun exploding or whatever, but suddenly there's an invasion of the undead. Luckily, you found this book in a bargain bin in your local bookshop. Inside it, there's a step-by-step guide to keeping yourself alive during the Zombie Apocalypse.

Rule 1 Find yourself a safe house.

Now's your chance to finally live in that expensive property you've always dreamed of. Prices no longer apply – it's finders keepers, losers weepers. Y'know that Lamborghini you've always wanted? That's yours, too.

Rule 2 Pop down to your local DIY store to pick up some much needed weaponry.

Anything that looks like it could kill you, could kill them. Use your imagination: a chainsaw would be even better if it was on fire, right? Have fun with it, you only live once … unless you're a zombie!

Rule 3 Dress yourself in mouldy flesh.

Even though people may think this attracts zombies it actually deflects them because it's fresh meat that they want. Mouldy flesh can be found on rotting corpses and dead zombies.

Rule 4 Find a partner who isn't dead.

Zombie girlfriends suck because they have nothing good to say and their body parts are usually pretty loose (if you know what I mean). Same goes for zombie boyfriends – all the Viagra in the world's not gonna help you there. Look for someone who is breathing and then concentrate on reproducing.

Rule 5 Don't be a prick.

Zombies didn't choose to be zombies, they were literally eaten alive. Kill those that try to kill you but don't be disrespectful.

OCTOBER TOUR - STEFAN

Touring is considered the rock star's dream – sex, drugs and long drives. In October 2010 we took to the passenger seats in an insane two weeks of motorways and sore throats. Dru and myself had done some tiny tours before this, but nothing major. This wasn't even a long tour but Ashley, who had barely played a note on his bass, couldn't have been further from his comfort zone. The boy rocked it, though, even if we had to tuck him in nice and early after each show. Dru and I, on the other hand, thought we'd show off with the little experience we had and tried to live the rock star life ... We failed of course.

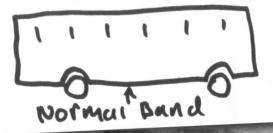

Normal Band

us

Drinking + Dancing = No to the next day

There is no way even Rambo or Rocky could wake up with a hangover, dance for 50 minutes on stage and not complain. But what's not to love about touring? You've already seen what a Midnight Beast rider looks like. A rider is a list you give to every venue that they HAVE to deliver on. You want Doritos? You got it. You want a 70" plasma TV screen? You got it. You want monkeys juggling flame-throwers? You got it! Well, maybe ...

Sometimes, though, touring isn't always what it's cracked up to be. There's a lot of sitting around and asking for wifi passwords so you can scour the Internet for porn. Luckily, one of the best forms of entertainment a band can have is their support act, and we chose Aggro Santos, who was a pleasure to have around.

Nathen + Me - Dank

Also, our awesome crew helped us get stuff done. The tall guy circled here is my uncle Jude. Nobody messes with us when Jude is around. If anyone ever tries to give us trouble, we give them one look at this fella and they're halfway back home with soggy pants. Of course he's a friendly giant really, though. One particular highlight of having Jude around is his sense of humour. I particularly remember the time I was signing some autographs for a group of female fans in Wales, and Jude casually comes over and asks me if I've remembered to use my thrush cream. Hilarious.

Fake Ashley

Kyle

LADS

KYLE

STEFAN'S GUIDE TO DANCE

As much as we love writing a good song, The Midnight Beast would not be what it is today without some erotic dance moves sprinkled on top. Breakdance, jazz, ballet, tap – we know it all and we've done it all. Ashley and I were learning dance from an early age, from my first run-in with breakdancing – which led to a hernia and a few weeks off school – to Ashley's being a tap guru at the age of 12. Even Dru's mum is a ballerina and she taught him everything he knows now. (This is not a lie; it can be seen just how graceful he is.)

Now let's get one thing straight: as much as it looks like we're randomly flailing our arms around, there is method to the madness.

Lesson 1 – FRIENDSHIP
Practise in front of friends. They will tell you when something looks shit.

Lesson 2 – DREAMS
Never give up your dreams ... I don't actually know what this means, but people always say it in films, so it must be true.

Lesson 3 – THE COMPETITION
Study the competition and beat the competition. Sometimes you must work on being better than them and sometimes you must work on breaking their legs. This is a competitive industry so don't let no muthafuckers stand in your way. You don't get nowhere in this life without smashing a few skulls – that's what Grandma taught me, anyway. It's a harsh reality and where others fail you must use their bones for oars in this sea of competition.

Lesson 4 – MUSIC VIDEO
Every dancer must be in a music video – it's like the Bible for dancers. Either get yourself a part in one or, failing that, steal yourself a part in one. They're usually shooting in your nearest city at night-time, so position yourself in the background of one of the cameras and shine, baby, SHINE!

Lesson 5 – TV TALENT
Nowadays the world is bloody crazy about dance. Reality dance shows are popping up all over the place. People have even made FILMS about dance (yeah, I know). Take advantage of the current hysteria and enter as many dance

competitions as you can. Make sure you're good, though, because these competitions can be televised and you'll end up making an absolute tit of yourself if you're rubbish.

Lesson 6 — COMMITMENT

Have you ever seen *Fame*? Those kids had commitment coming out of their arses. You better show those babies what you got inside of you. Do you wanna live forever? Do you wanna learn how to fly, HIGH? Do you feel it coming together? People will see you and cry *FAME*! Yeah, that's right, if in doubt just quote lyrics from '80s films. It works for me.

Lesson 7 — OUTFITS

Costumes, clothes – whatever you want to call them – are the most important thing for a dancer. They will make you stand out. Sparkles, glitter, meats – these are all things you could try covering your favourite leotard in – the brighter, the better.

Lesson 8 — MOVES

Make sure you know what to do with your body. Study videotapes of EVERYTHING. From Lady Gaga to giraffes, ice skating to horse racing: dancing is everywhere. Maybe base yourself on the way an ostrich moves. Or run around squawking like a seagull.

Lesson 9 — MUSIC

Did you ever think for one second you could get away without dancing to music? FUCK THAT. Pick your favourite song and play it backwards, or take your five best songs and make a mega-mix, put in some robot sounds too, like 'BSSSH, BEEEP, BWAAARRRRP', and then move your body like an actual robot. You'll have the judges of any competition you enter pissing themselves with excitement.

Lesson 10 — USP

That means Unique Selling Point for those of you that don't watch *The Apprentice*. Whether you're always dressed as a tiger, or if whenever you dance there's always a strange smell of methane gas, you need something that will make you stand out. Ask friends and family what works for you. I remember once watching a young female dancer and at the end she pulled her pants down and she had a man-stick. Come to think about it, I don't think that was a dance show, actually.

FAIL

THE OCTOBER TOUR
SELL-OUTS BY ASH

Being in a comedy band is a hard life. The average day goes
something like this:
sleep in until 10 a.m., have salmon and eggs for breakfast,
go to the gym, indulge in a liquid lunch, write a few
sketches or songs, eat a three-course dinner, watch
Entourage, play Xbox until 2 a.m. and then wake up to the
sound of Playboy TV from the night before. Good times.
There is a point where all of this has to stop though. You
have to leave it behind ... and go on tour.

Go on tour? Being a mere actor, I have never endured the
experience of touring with a band. I thought I would
have to prepare myself for drug-taking, partying 24/7,
consuming ungodly amounts of alcohol and hanging out
with groupies. But then again, The Midnight Beast is the
uncoolest group known to man.

The average day on tour goes something like this:
wake up at around 7 a.m. due to Dru's snoring,
squabble over who gets the first shower (quick
note – we may have sold out our first tour, but me,
Stefan and Andrew still had to share a family
room at the Travelodge), head over to the tour
van, wait a good half an hour extra for our
dancers to glam themselves up, grab breakfast –
if we could stomach it – drive for a few hours, tell
a few penis and bum jokes, get carsick, stop at a
service station on the verge of pissing my pants,
drive a few more hours and finally arrive at the

venue. It's always a great feeling to reach our destination after spending a couple of hours in a tight space with a group of guys – you can only imagine what smells are created. When we get there we meet and greet with hard-core fans who have waited outside in the cold since the early hours of the morning and then after that it's time to chow down on our very bad-boy rider – no alcohol for me, just a warm juice and a sandwich.

It's SHOWTIME

The crowd flood the venue and we are ready to roll. During those 45 minutes you could compare me to an out of control firework, a dangerous mover who is too hot to handle. ;)

I tend to celebrate a triumphant gig with a glass of water and a banana, then head to the stage door for more meet and greets with everyone who has made the effort to come and see the Beast. In Manchester there were hundreds chanting 'Midnight Beast' at our dressing-room window and it was HAVOC. I made the most of the situation and dangled a plastic baby doll out of the window, inspired by Michael Jackson. After the gig we would head straight back to the hotel for a herbal tea, and I would prepare myself for another sleepless night thanks to the sound of Andrew's nostrils.

Almost as soon as the road trip had started, it was time to head back home. What did I learn from this tour? I desperately attempted to be a rock star, but failed. I am not rock 'n' roll: I just rock and then roll into bed, with my night trousers and a hot mug of cocoa.

Agony Aunt

ASK ASH

'Alright Ash, David 'ere from Essex. I 'ave bin with my girlfriend for a few years, but recently I have developed an attraction to playing with My Little Pony, more so than 'er. When Chantelle offers a bit of "sexy time", I would rather turn my nose up at that, head to my attic and go on a magical adventure with my Pink Princess, "Dream". How can I save my relationship?'

Hello David,

Firstly, I would like to declare I also had the same problem a few years back. It drove my girlfriend insane and she sadly left me. There is something so playful and fun about these four-legged bundles of joy, but there comes a time when it must stop. I would advise you gather all your stallion demons into a pile outside, sprinkle a few litres of petrol over their adorable faces, light a match and BURN THOSE EVIL BIATCHES TO THE GROUND. Do it as quickly as you can or they will ruin you! Big Love Bro, Ash

Good day to you, Sir Horne the Ladykiller, fellow Earth dweller. I am Arathor, protector of the Seven Kingdoms, level 24. I am in need of some much needed assistance regarding a fair young maiden I am trying to win the hand of. How does one triumph in such a quest?

Greetings young knight, thou shall only impress such a fine specimen if thou is level 30: own a fucking Ferrari, have pockets as deep as Amsterdam's finest, and brush up on your social skills, you weirdo. Leave the realm known as your bedroom, put on a shirt and start the adventure of LIFE. The End.

IF THE MIDNIGHT BEAST MADE PARTIES (THEY WOULD BE THE BEST PARTIES EVER)

Here's a lesson why by your boy Stefan ... **PARTAA** !

P is for People who don't party like us. You could say we put the 'art' in 'Partaay'. I remember Dru and I partied so hard one New Year's Eve that we forgot to find a bed. So I used his body as a pillow whilst he slept on the cold stony kitchen floor ... WHAT A GUY.

A is for After the party. There's ALWAYS an after party and then after that there's an after after party, and so on. We never know how to stop.

R is for Riding home from a party in a trolley. This is always how the night ends. Why walk when you can vandalise the streets AND sit down the whole way home? I once saw Dru nearly break his neck when he and our friend AJ clambered on and the poor trolley collapsed ... Oh, good times.

T is for Terrible breath, which will never get you laid at a party when the Fat Lady sings and it is time to hook up with somebody. Always brush your teeth before leaving the house.

A is for Alcohol. And if you want your host to like you, bring plenty of it. A party ain't a party without a keg of beer. I don't even drink beer but I take a keg everywhere I go – if anything, just to look cool.

A is for Ask your parents about their childhood and all the stuff they got up to. Sometimes they've even got good advice about how to get laid or fucked up.

Y is for Yes is the best rule to play by, but sometimes it's good to know when to say no.
'Hey Stefan, wanna jump in the pool?'
'Yes.'
'Hey Stefan, wanna touch the horse's penis with a stick?'
'Yes.'
'Hey Stefan, wanna touch my penis with a stick?'
'No thank you. You're a good friend, ~~Ashley~~, but I would not like to do that.'

Dru

84

NICE SMILE

83

I.AM.HORNEY'S DANCE MOVES

My name is Ashley Neil Horne and I am more wanted than top-shelf porn. FACT. Want to know why? Well, move over Michael Flatley, the new Lord of the Dance is in town. I have more rhythm in my small toe than John Travolta. Here's a few tips on how to move like me, I.Am.Horney, better known as Swivel Hips.

1. **Diet.** This helps BIG time if you want to move like a pro. I recommend a few Creme Eggs for breakfast. Eggs are rich in vitamins, protein and fats – this is proven by nutritionists. Lunch should be a light salad: a lettuce leaf, slice of cucumber and one tomato, then pour on bucketloads of salad dressing. Dinner consists of any kind of energy bar or drink – it will give you that extra boost to dance the night away!

2. **Loosen up.** You must prepare yourself for a hard night of finely executed moves, so be nimble, be sharp and do stretches. Turn on some classic '80s montage music, feel the rhythm and get to it! I recommend 'You're the Best' by Joe Esposito or 'Eye of the Tiger'.

3. **So you think you can dance?** The best moves are the ones that cause people to react – no matter what the reaction is. It means they are paying attention to your unique style. Classic I.Am.Horney moves include pit-thrusts, head-nods, head-rolls, eye-rolls, head-spins, finger-spins, knee-spins, needless arm-throws-in-the-air and fast turns with eyes closed. Do all this and I might have some competition ... only joking, you suck compared to me. I AM A WINNER. COCK

DRU'S GUIDE TO DANCE

'One, two, three, four. Step, two, three, four.'

As you should all be aware by now, I am an exceptional ballet dancer. Yes, that's right, the man with the fuzzy beard whose every other utterance contains the word 'twat' can be as graceful as a swan, just like in *Swan Lake*. For those of you less familiar with the arts, that's a pretty famous ballet (and in fact my mum danced in *Swan Lake* in her youth). You see, my mum taught me everything I know about the world of ballet and I thought I would now pass my knowledge on to you.

Step 1: DON'T BE A PRICK

No one likes an arrogant, know-it-all arsehole who thinks they are God's gift. So whether you're in a squad, company, group or taking lessons, try and make some friends. It makes things like lifts a lot easier when you have them.

Step 2: WARM UP/STRETCH

It's an absolute must! I have suffered shin splints before from not doing a warm-up and it fucking hurts. Gammy legs, hernias and bunions are also common occurrences in the world of ballet. Nice.

Step 3: HAVE A POO

You just don't do dance on a full stomach. You wouldn't want to be downwind of somebody who lets a fart slip whilst they're holding in a big poo and they wouldn't appreciate it from you, either.

Step 4: KEEP COUNT

It does kind of help if you can count – otherwise
how will you know where you are in the song/piece?

Step 5: LEARN YOUR POSITIONS

There are five positions you must know and learn in ballet:
The first position is feet together but turned out.
The second position is the feet turned out but now apart.
The third is when one foot is in front of the other, turned out
with the heel of the front foot touching (in line with the arch of
the foot behind).
The fourth is the same positioning of the feet as the third,
but the feet are apart so that the front foot is further forward
than the back foot.
The fifth is also similar to the third but the front foot is pulled
further across so the heel of the front foot is in line with the
big toe of the foot behind.

Are you still with me?!

Finally, the sixth step is where you
stretch your arms from your
chest outwards and as you do
so you flop your head down
and inwards in a sort of
swooshing motion.

That's all there is to it.
You can now do ballet.

FIT!

JUST ANOTHER
B★YBAND

BRIAN BISHOP AS THE PRODUCER

JOSE GUTIERREZ AS THE A&R

LARRY LEBZELTER AS THE MANAGER

JAB

BOYBAND AUDITIONS

A/S/L
AGE/SEX/LOCATION

Boy bands tend to do this thing where they answer lots of small stupid pointless questions, but for some reason, people like to know all the answers. We have decided to do a similar thing ... so here is a side to The Midnight Beast you didn't know.

NAME: Stefan James Donald John Abingdon
AGE: 22
SEX: Yes please
LOCATION: Earth
NICKNAME: Curly-top/Stabadabadingdong
FAVE COLOUR: Black
FAVE FOOD: McChicken Nuggets
FAVE FILM: *The Lion King*
FAVE ANIMAL: Hyena
FAVE TEAM: Team Edward (til I die)
FAVE JOKE: Ashley
FAVE FRUIT: Onion
FAVE SANDWICH: Peanut butter and jelly and grape
FAVE WEATHER: Snow
FAVE DRINK: Water
FAVE SONG: 'Trailer Park Jesus' by GlassJaw
FAVE CAR: Taxi
FAVE CELEB: Andre 3000
TURN ON: Music
TURN OFF: Stopping music
KISS: Buffy the Vampire Slayer
MARRY: Mischa Barton
KILL: Pointless patronising children's comedy
DATE: A beach stroll at dusk

MOCK STARS

As strange as it is to think, celebrities are just people too.
We've met a few famous people in our career from The Misfits
at C4's Comedy Gala to Chipmunk at BBC Radio One. I suppose
in some people's eyes we're celebrities too ... and that's plain
ridiculous because I'm writing this whilst picking my nose in
the back of my parents' people carrier.

It's weird when we find out people we respect, or people we have
been watching since we were kids, like our stuff. Frank Skinner,
Michael McIntyre and James Corden all count themselves as fans of The
Midnight Beast. Jonathan Ross even invited us round for his
Hallowe'en party. It's also odd getting noticed by groups of people
whilst you're just out and about: we turned up to do a DJ set in Wales and
were welcomed like we were the Beatles. But it never gets old. In fact,
one of my fondest memories is running into a secluded pub after being
mobbed at a Paramore show while Ashley and Dru remained
surrounded by confused fans thinking they were Justin
Bieber and the drummer from Paramore. One girl
even gave Dru a toy to give to Hayley
Williams ... It's an odd life being Mock
Stars, but my God we love it.

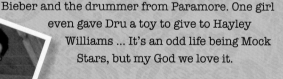

THE MIDNIGHT BEAST'S GUIDE TO LONDON

London is a big, scary place filled with big and scary people, so if you've never visited it or maybe if you've visited it once and ended up cowering in one of those red phone boxes that nobody uses because they're actually toilets and smell like piss, you might want to take a look at our guide.

Stefan's tour of the best tourist attractions

London has loads of history so you're gonna need to sort the good tourist attractions from the bad ones.

Thorpe Park is a theme park situated just outside London and it has been there for hundreds of years. Actually one of the queens opened it ages ago so it is an absolute must-see.

There is a massive clock next to one of the many bridges. It's actually just a normal clock and doesn't do anything that another clock can't, and in fact rumour has it that the clock inside it is the size of a wristwatch. It isn't actually that big, except compared to the rest of London, which it towers above ... it's called **Big Ben**.

There are many amazing buildings in London that look awesome from the outside but inside they're used for really boring stuff – a bit like Sarah Palin. The **Gherkin** is a prime example, just take a look at it ...

AWESOME! Do you know what that is? Some kind of office block.

How to be a Londoner by Ash

LAAAANDAAAAAAN, the beautiful capital city of Britain.

Litter literally litters the streets, fast food smells fill the nostrils, tourists block the pavement happy-snapping at pointless objects, gladiators battle to give out free newspapers, you have to pay a fortune for a packet of crisps, and pigeons spread disease ... what is there not to love?

If you wanna fit in with the 'cool kids' around London there are a few things you have to do:

It's all about Me, Me, Me

Speaking LOUDLY is a must. Whenever you are in conversation with anyone you must let the WHOLE world know what you are talking about. It would be rude not to.

Swagger

Everyone in London has somewhere to be. Walk around with an air of arrogance and if anyone gets in your way, knock them down. Remember they are in the wrong by blocking you from reaching your destination. Wankers.

Deep thinker

Get your laptop out and head for the busiest central coffee shop you can find. If you are writing your latest novel or script or just browsing on the Book of Face, make sure you do it in a public place or no one will believe how intellectual you are. Honestly.

'Ave a Larf

Going out in Laaaandan is all about living like there is no tomorrow. Get smashed off your tits and pull some fit bird. It's not been a good night until you've been sick in the street. You might even finish the night off with a fight and if you're lucky enough, end up in a comfy bed in A&E. Look at it as a free hotel. Scooore!!

Dru turns tour guide

'London's burning, London's burning ...'

Don't worry, London isn't burning any more! It hasn't been for quite a few years now. It did once, because of a silly baker man who decided to have forty winks whilst leaving the bloody oven on (I won't mention names). Rest assured we have learnt from our mistakes and now have a pretty good fire brigade service. But aside from tales of big fires that nearly engulfed a whole city and a rather iconic fire brigade, London has some pretty sick attractions and places to visit, or hang – do people hang any more? Let's go with hang all the same.

My first sightseeing suggestion is **the London Underground**. To many tourists – and let's face it, Londoners too – the underground is a rather daunting mode of transport.

It's dark, hot, sweaty, slow and it can also smell of piss sometimes, let alone the fact that it can be fucking confusing! I think they even had to get some artist guy to draw out the different lines and stations so that it was easier to read and understand. Nonetheless, it's still an absolute must to have a token picture of you beside a London Underground sign.

From the tube we move on to ... a ship. No, that isn't a typo, **HMS *Belfast*** is my next suggestion in my guide to London. The clue is in the name, but this ship is no ordinary ship. It served in some war, maybe a few, I've forgotten, but now it lives beside Tower Bridge and is actually treated as a museum. From standing on the deck pretending you're captain (ooh kinky), to walking around the pit where they load the heavy guns – you can do it all. At one point you even used to be able to sit on a smaller gun on deck and move it around, pretending you were shooting aeroplanes rather than harmlessly pointing it at seagulls and pigeons.

With all that touristy stuff seen to, let's talk about London's night life. Some parts of this city contain one-off clubs, bars and one-of-a-kind pubs. Some however, will contain the same shitty pubs and clubs that are part of an awful chain. Fights, football hooligans and drugs can be a common occurrence in this particular scene but don't let that put you off – after all this is London, that sort of shit can kick off at any point!

STEFAN TALKS ABOUT PLAYING AT THE COMEDY AWARDS

When we were asked to perform at the C4 Comedy Awards we were all too happy to say yes. We were told that because we were performing at the after party we would not need any suits but this wasn't quite true as we were forced to walk down the red carpet in our makeshift smart/casualwear. Dru wore a hoody, Ashley wore a leather jacket, I wore a full suit and my dad's shirt and my dad (who was accompanying us on the night) wore a nice black suit with BROWN shoes! We looked like an eyesore but we walked down the red carpet with pride, even if nobody knew who we were. We even got stuck behind Rob Brydon whilst he was getting papped.

We were ushered from the red carpet to our seats and watched some familiar faces receive awards that we can only hope one day to sniff from the front row ... maybe even touch with our sticky fingers. Halfway through the second advert break we were rushed upstairs to take our position in a room which housed the casts of *Misfits*, *The Inbetweeners* and *Fonejacker*, Simon Le Bon out of Duran Duran and a few more familiar faces, all being followed around by clingers-on. We were dressed in our usual colourful clothes and clutching coloured pompoms, so naturally people turned to have a look. We'd met *The Inbetweeners* before so we managed to whimper around behind them for a while before going live on TV. Louis Spence was there getting pissed off because his interview might get cut for three male cheerleaders singing about a 'Booty Call', but we embraced the attention and went for it ... I even flipped over the sofa for a nice dramatic finish. We later found out it didn't make the final cut. You'll find this particular performance on the Internet somewhere ... Have you heard about the Internet? It's really good.

USE YA HEAD

The Midnight Beast had been alive for over a year now so a song about SEX was long overdue and it was time to charge up our dirty minds. A real charity, Marie Stopes, asked if we three beasts wanted to front their safe sex campaign and little did they know our lyrics would cause such an uproar. We have plenty enough smutty ideas to write a ten-minute song just on bondage and other kinky things. But after much thought, we put our fantasies to one side and started to brainstorm a song that would appeal to the masses, not just three perverted young boys. Around the same time, JLS (a really cool boy band: Merton, Ascot, Big J and the other one) had a stroke of genius to release their own brand of condoms in a range of different sizes... I wonder which member had been given the extra small? JLS wanted to promote safe sex and I have no doubt they succeeded, but would any sane guy want to put Merton's face on the helm of their knob? We were inspired: 'Use Ya Head' was born.

Finely dressed in our retro attire we messed around with dildos, blow-up dolls, handcuffs and lube. It was just another normal day for Dru, Ash and Stef. I even had a casual cock-slip, which, obviously, was caught on camera and straight away uploaded to Twitter. Oh the calamity.

After a little bit of hard work and lots of immature antics, the video was posted up on the World Wide Web. Boy, did it kick up a storm. BAM! 'Use Ya Head' was front page of the *Metro*. They picked up on the line 'One up the bum, and you won't be a mum,' claiming that Marie Stopes – via TMB – was actually promoting anal sex as a way of averting pregnancy. Comedy gold. The next morning we were the topic of discussion on *The Wright Stuff*. They shot us down as silly kids with the intention of promoting anal sex. We couldn't see why they were clearly ignoring the end quote on our video: 'DO NOT TRUST THE MIDNIGHT BEAST WITH SAFE SEX ADVICE.' On and on they went, having a dig at The Midnight Beast, completely unaware of who we – or more importantly, our fans – were. Thousands of comments were left on *The Wright Stuff* webshite, declaring how ignorant a guy on the panel was. Later that day he apologised via Twitter. What an absolute bumder ...

100

SCHOOL REPORT

Pupil name: Andrew Wakely

Andrew Wakely is a bright young lad with great potential. Although he has been suspended numerous times for his use of profanity, spraying graffiti on school property, smoking illegal substances in the locker room and starting a riot in his lunch break, he always finds a way to convince us to not expel him, due to his shining sense of humour.

Andrew has shown a real interest in Science, especially when it comes to chemicals. He has studied in-depth the creation and history of Calpol. He also has a real flair for poetry – a poem called 'Daddy' managed to get him our Star Pupil Award, which is only given out to the most inspiring young writers.

Overall, Andrew is a fine pupil. I have been asked to remove Andrew from class multiple times for tapping on tables, but I understand this is only due to his active musical mind. I really do wish him the best of luck in the future and hope he learns to control his anger problems before they start controlling him!

Yours sincerely,

Mr Abingdon
(Headmaster)

A/S/L?

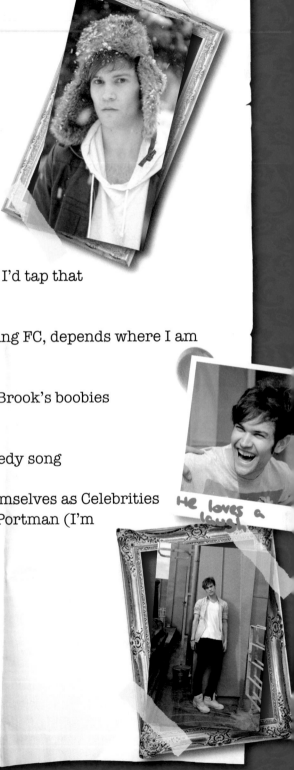

NAME: Ashley Neil Horne
AGE: 22
SEX: Male
LOCATION: Putney, AKA Putters
NICKNAME: Smash, AshBash, Ashbashflashgash
FAVE COLOUR: Blue, like my tears
FAVE FILM: Anything with Mila Kunis, I'd tap that
FAVE FOOD: Salmon
FAVE ANIMAL: Monkey
FAVE TEAM: Newcastle United or Reading FC, depends where I am
FAVE JOKE: Stefan's hair
FAVE FRUIT: Pineapple
FAVE SANDWICH: Me in between Kelly Brook's boobies
FAVE WEATHER: Smog
FAVE DRINK: A water vodka
FAVE SONG: Anything that isn't a comedy song
FAVE CAR: Jaguar. Meow.
FAVE CELEB: The ones who refer to themselves as Celebrities
TURN ON: Mila Kunis kissing Natalie Portman (I'm just watching)
TURN OFF: Kerry Katona
KISS: Girls
MARRY: Super Hot Girls
KILL: Kerry Katona's career
DATE: Birthday

He loves a laugh

FEBRUARY TOUR BY DRU

SOLD OUT!

TUESDAY 15th FEBRUARY
PORTSMOUTH WEDGEWOOD ROOMS

BOOM!

'We sold out another tour?'

We already had our first sold-out tour under our belts and then before we knew it we were off on a second! We started off in sunny Fulham where we gathered at Stefan's place – and there the hilarities and calamities started. Straight away the Flip camera came out and people were messing around with drawn-on eyes on a plastic case, sweets, Stefan was making amusing little raps and there was general pissing about in the back of the van.

BOOM! After a little drive we landed in **Portsmouth** with Stefan singing a bloody song by Bieber and Ashley claiming I wasn't funny any more. Cheers, dude. We didn't wanna set up the gear straight away when we arrived at the venue, so instead we played a spot of badminton. I was pretty shit at it. After singing and dancing backstage to 'Heavy' by Chase and Status and 'Drop the World' By Lil Wayne and Eminem, it was time to rock out on the first night of the tour – and my God did we rock out. Portsmouth certainly made the first night one to remember.

We then hit **Birmingham**, where badminton was replaced with spacehoppers and little scooters that we took on the road with us for the shows. I fell over mine and was just pleased the moment wasn't caught on camera – at least not as far as I know. My ears were still ringing long after the Birmingham show. It was crazy listening as the crowd sang and rapped their way through 'Ninjas': we didn't really even need to join in. When we got offstage Ashley claimed he was feeling ' fucking rock and roll' and the dressing room started to look like it. It soon turned into a bit of a party.

Caught

With Hype Man Sage and his DJ (and personal friend of mine) Mike Kruger with us for the ride, it was definitely gonna get rowdy! The JD was flowing and we enjoyed any drinks we could find. It was also our mate's birthday, so after singing him a rendition of ' Happy Birthday' we decided to stick around at the venue when it turned into a club. We got lost that night on the way home but through sheer determination and the help of the shining lights of our Travelodge, we made it.

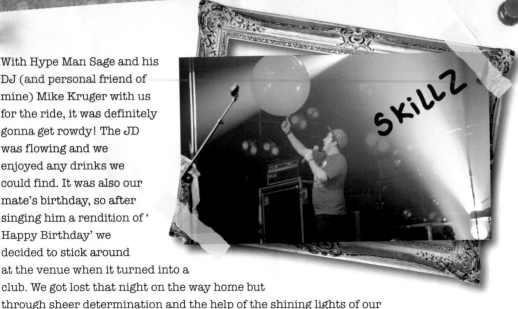

SKILLZ

Next on our tour was **Liverpool**, home to the mighty Joe Setz ... and the Beatles, too, of course. It was BLOODY COLD but the show was absolutely nuts and so much fun. Stef got so excited afterwards that he tore off his shirt and swung it around and around. We played a game called The Floor is Made of Lava – where you can only stand, walk and climb on chairs and tables – it's pretty fun, you should try it! After the show it seemed like literally the whole crowd was waiting outside, which was awesome. Mind you, somebody tried to nick my Strongbow, and nobody nicks Dru's Strongbow, OK?!

On the day that we headed to **Sheffield**, I received tweets from people who had been outside the venue since 8 a.m. in the morning. Now that is insane but amazing, and we love you for it! The mentalness soon kicked off backstage. We all started to go a little mad listening to Limp Bizkit, kicking chairs over and pelvic thrusting like no end. Man, I wish Fred Durst could have seen us!

Natural Muscles

Next up, the home of Ashley's favourite football team ... **Newcastle**! After a car journey with Ash the entire time trying to explain to Stefan what offside was in football, we arrived at the venue. It was during a pre-show Sunday roast that we learned that Ashley's favourite bands are Keane and Coldplay! Cooooooool!

FACT: In **Edinburgh** they don't call a full English breakfast a 'Full English', it's a 'Full Scottish'. And quite right too. So Edinburgh was the next stop on the tour and like all the shows on the tour, Edinburgh certainly knows how to make some noise. It was definitely a fun show to play, although I think it was at this point that all three of us started to catch little colds and get sore throats. As if we were gonna let that stop us from partying – the show must go on!

In **Norwich** we were about to play on the same stage as Roll Deep and it was going to be a night to remember – partly because Stef had a go at playing drums but mainly because he was too busy looking back at me as he walked off and fell off the stage. A bit of wee nearly came out when that happened.

With a few star jumps and a vocal warm-up under our belts, we headed out to try and 'entertain' Norwich ... I think we succeeded :)

Last but not least was the big finale. We were headlining at KOKO! This was a very exciting experience as it was the biggest venue we had played so far, let alone that we had headlined, and when we arrived there was such a long queue all the way around the venue that we couldn't unload our stuff. The last time we had stepped out on to this stage was to support the mighty Hadouken! boys, and that was only a three-song set. It was crazy to think that we were already headlining with a full set. The show was also amazing. When we came offstage we were all still stunned at what had just happened. It was not only an amazing show but a sick-ass tour and we met some amazing people on the way! Huge thank you to everyone that came to the shows, we love you all!

ASHLEY'S TIPS ON HOW TO END A RELATIONSHIP

It's a Friday night, the feeling's right, you know what time it is ...
SEXY TIME. You've put on some Tom Jones, sprinkled the
bed with red rose petals and lit the room with scented candles. Wow,
you're slick. The scene is set, your girlfriend or boyfriend will be in
any minute now, the door opens ... and your partner stumbles in
drunk, mutters a few swear words, falls on the bed and goes on to
wet themselves. **ZZZZZZZZZZZZZ**. It's time for a change,
time to end this relation-shit. (Check out my witty play with words.)
But how do you get rid of the extra luggage? I will tell you how.

You know I'm only gonna break your heart .... right?

1. Happy birthday, you're dumped

The most respected way to end a relationship is via email or text. Twitter is the new cool thing, so why not break the news over a trendy website? Alternatively, wait until a big event in the calendar comes aknocking: Christmas, birthday or a patron saint's day. Write your break-up message in a card and send it off. Your ex-lover might be upset over the split but on the good side, they will end up with a lovely festive card.

2. Can't touch this

Simple as it may seem, just disappear. Instantly detach yourself from the whereabouts of your ex and they will completely forget about you, losing all memory of your time together. It honestly works, believe me, my ex suddenly disappeared one night and I never saw or heard from her again!

3. Showdown

Invite a few hot ladies round while your girlfriend is in your house. Wait until your partner is in the same room and then, **WHAM BAM**, snog one of the smoking hot women in front of her eyes. This should go down a treat.

4. One-liner

If you fail to do any of the above, just use the simple yet effective line:
'We're over. It's you, not me.'

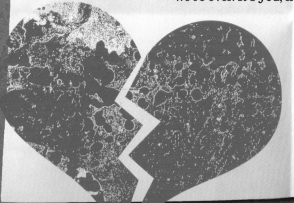

There is no need to thank me for my golden advice, just thank God for making Ashley Neil Horne such a talented and clever individual.

FEBRUARY TOUR

It's February 2011, we've already got one tour under our belt and as quickly as we could say 'We're announcing another tour' it had sold out. We'd spent days thinking 'Can we do it again? Was the last one just a fluke?' and now it was time to hit the road.

We packed our bags and left our weeping mothers behind, getting into a van full of a nice manly crew, with a few new faces, too. I say a van, but for this tour we actually travelled separately in my brother's car for two reasons: 1) We thought we could play a trick on the early showgoers when we rocked up in a decoy vehicle ... it didn't work out – we got spotted just as easily, maybe due to the curly hat hair, familiar eyebrows and shaggy beard. And 2) We thought we'd have more relaxing journeys ... more relaxing what?! Sitting in a car with Ashley and Dru is hardly relaxing. It's like calling a bullfight relaxing. The hyperactivity never ends in this band so we made a pact – a big energy-drink pact to never slow down until death.

Now this tour was bigger (by a day or so) and we didn't have any home stops so it was go go go! I made sure to pack lots of boxers because I knew it'd get rowdy. We soon found ourselves at venues bigger than we could possibly imagine and nearly as soon as it had started it was time to go home.

SCHOOL REPORT

Pupil: Ashley Horne

Overall:

Ashley Horne has been a pleasure to teach this term. He has showed a polite manner towards the other members of staff and also to his peers (although he perhaps enjoys the company of certain female peers a little too much on occasion).

Workwise, he has excelled on all counts. However, he does slightly lack on the homework front from time to time. Ashley has, on more than one occasion, turned up with the same piece of homework that he appears to have copied from another particular student word for word. Each time he claims he can't understand how, saying he 'did it at home'!

Aside from this Ashley has been in on time consistently and is rarely absent from school.

Areas For Improvement:

Aside from having a good year there are some improvements to be made, homework being one of them. It is unacceptable to be copying someone else's work. Another area for improvement is Food Technology: Ashley has been taking part but more care, awareness and general understanding of cooking hygiene and basic skills are needed. When he was set the task of researching and preparing a meal, I found him looking up local Italian restaurants. When challenged to do something on his own he presented a rather bland rice ... and that was it. More thought and research is needed as this was not the hardest task Ashley has faced this year.

Music Technology: Ashley has taken the 'I can't do it, so therefore I won't bother' approach. When asked to pick an instrument to study, he made his choice by asking friends what a cool one to play would be. He went through a phase of playing the drums, guitar and even the glockenspiel. Due to his indecision, he has been left weeks behind everyone else. After settling down with the bass guitar on my instruction, he stopped practising after just week three. It's a real shame as I saw, for a brief second, a slight glimpse of talent there.

Signed:

Mr D Wakely

GROWING DOWN
(TEENAGE REBELLION)

I've been alive for 22 years so I've been through my rebellious patch and (I think) come out the other side. My parents were not at all strict so I hardly had much to rebel against; all I used to want to do was play pop-punk in Dru's living room. We used to play at Wimbledon Community Centre at a club called MeMu that was set up by the local schools. Getting drunk was a huge deal when I was 14, and when I recently went to LA all the kids there were shocked when I told them what a massive part of growing up drinking a bottle of vodka with your friends in a park or on a common was. They couldn't understand it and looking back I don't understand why it was such a big deal now, either. But some funny stuff happened back then so I'm going to spill some disjointed memories of my youth for you to laugh, cry or get annoyed about ...

I remember going to a party in a graveyard with my friends who were all older than me and one of them broke his ankle jumping off a wall. I also remember one of those friends told everybody that he got all his front teeth kicked out by a local gang and when the dentist was repairing his teeth he asked if he wanted a satellite dish put in so he could listen to the radio. Why do these kids exist in every friendship group?! The same guy used to be in an old band of mine too, until Dru threw him out. I remember constantly being harassed by chavs, pikies, or whatever else you might call them. One group stole my chips in Kingston. I also remember organising fights that would never happen between the rockers and the chavs. I once smoked a homemade bong on my friend's trampoline and threw up all over his garden; and I remember going on dates with girls from Putney High to

Wimbledon cinema (so we wouldn't have to speak), and if they held my hand I'd tell all my friends about it.

I remember Halloween when a gang of boys in *Scream* masks mugged Dru and one of the boys said, 'Sorry, it's my first time,' and I recall my only way to get a girl to like me would be to write a song about her and invite her to watch my band play, except sometimes the sound would be bad and I'd sing the whole thing completely out of tune and at the end be faced with her confused expression. I once got high to impress some older boys and forgot who my parents were and what my name was, and burst out crying. I also remember going for a piss on Wimbledon Common, running into a tree eye-first and knocking myself out. I remember when Dru and his mate AJ posted a video of them doing Ricky Gervais impressions and they had to take it down because it got so much Internet abuse, and I won't forget when I had to see the principal of my school because I pointed at some poo in the street and said to a boy in my class, 'That's you, that is.' I remember when a boy from another school spat Kebab all over my blazer when I was walking home from school one night, and the time when I got three detentions because I hated my Spanish teacher and told her so in front of my class. I remember when I bought a FUBU tracksuit and red goggles because I wanted to look like Ali G and didn't understand the irony. How could I ever forget when a friend (who won't be named) tried to have sex with the suction pipe in a swimming pool in France? I remember crying with happiness the first time I went to Toys 'R' Us, and I remember crying with sadness because I was the only boy in south-west London that didn't get off with the slut down the road. I remember when my friend got me muddled up with the guy he was fighting and repeatedly punched me in the balls, and I also remember when I was nine that I fancied a girl so much that she spat in my cereal one morning and I still ate it. I remember spilling a bottle of beer on Adele's shoe. I remember when one of my best friends at school kept getting an erection when he stayed the night at my house and a couple weeks later he came out ... I wondered why he always used to want to wrestle with me.

Luckily I'm living a really normal life now and not doing anything out of the ordinary. Nothing whatsoever.

by Stefan

111

THE FEBRUARY TOUR BY ASHLEY

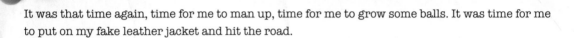

It was that time again, time for me to man up, time for me to grow some balls. It was time for me to put on my fake leather jacket and hit the road.

After our October tour, I now knew how to prepare for this kind of adventure. I had yoghurt bars (for those early mornings), Lemsip (for a hug in a mug), spray to numb my throat, extra pants, extra socks, a comfy pillow (on which to rest my weary head at night), thick honey and gallons of extra-strong water – everything a rock 'n' roll star needs.

This time we were also joined by some fresh faces: our support act, Hype Man Sage, a lovely young man who drove our crowd WILD to the sound of his twist on drum and bass; TMB's props and wardrobe guy, Elliot Tattler, a funny fucker who literally was a joke a minute – what a treat – and finally Joe Setz, a cheeky-chappy rapper from Liverpool who caused a storm at our final gig at KOKO in Camden.

The Midnight Beast was the fastest unsigned band to sell out KOKO, and soon after that the WHOLE tour was SOLD OUT. CRAZAY SHIT. At every venue we would be welcomed by beasts who eagerly awaited our arrival. Some would wait there for eight hours at a time – now that's dedication. Me, Dru and Stef were showered with gifts and you would not believe how many My Little Ponies I have been given: I have so many of them, it would make any girl think twice before stepping inside my bedroom. Thanks, guys.

Over the course of the tour I had developed man flu so my voice was slowly deteriorating. I was comforted with advice on how to tackle the problem. Here are some of the methods I was so wisely given:

1) Smother your chest with mustard

Now, I have an insane addiction to mustard but this is taking it a bit too far ... even for Mr Mustard.

2) Eat raw garlic

Never done it, never will.

3) Make a honey and onion cough elixir

This sounds too complicated, even for Harry Potter.

4) Put a hairless dog on your bare chest

I wasn't sure of the amount of time it must be upon my chest ... but I knew that at some point it would need to release its bowels.

5) Increase the moisture in the air around you

Pardon?

6) Eat pigeon soup

Disease in food form? No thanks.

7) Mix together goose grease and turpentine then rub it on your chest

I'm far too lazy to do this.

8) Get drunk

For goodness' sake, who drinks alcohol on tour? Professionalism, please.

9) Diffuse oil of oregano

Not entirely sure what that means.

10) Eat honey

Eat honey? Now we're talking. For the next two weeks I transformed into Winnie the Pooh. All I would eat was honey. Honey on toast, honey burgers, honey chips, honey mixed in Coke, honey on paper, honey on honey ... I would drizzle honey on to anything edible. I am still having counselling to part with this horrid addiction. It's hard, but Dr Honey, I mean Dr Boney, says I am making great progress.

We had come to the end of our tour and it was time to headline London's KOKO on the last night. KOKO is a venue I would go to as a kid and I could only dream of playing there (sick in mouth) ... let alone selling it out in under two days. We touched down outside the stage door and quick as a flash, swarms of beasts huddled around our van. When we made it into our dressing room, we could hear our songs being sung by the people down below. Before the gig started, me, Dru and Stef ventured to the front balcony of the venue and spoke to the crowd via megaphone. We were greeted with 1500+ cheers and it was one of the best feelings I have ever had. It was time to smash KOKO to shreds.

The February tour was now over, what to do next? Conquer the world? Maybe next year ...

A/S/L

NAME: Andrew Wakely
AGE: 24
SEX: Male
LOCATION: South-west London
NICKNAME: Dru
FAVE COLOUR: Any, really
FAVE FOOD: Wheat-free carbonara
FAVE FILM: *Law Abiding Citizen/Fight Club/Fast & Furious* - fuck yeah!
FAVE ANIMAL: Cats
FAVE TEAM: Team Dru
FAVE JOKE: 'I'm pregnant'
FAVE FRUIT: Strawberries
FAVE SANDWICH: Ham and cheese
FAVE WEATHER: Snow
FAVE DRINK: Strongbow/JD
FAVE SONG: Anything that's not quirky indie!
FAVE CAR: Mistubishi Evo
FAVE CELEB: Travis Barker
TURN ON: Girls
TURN OFF: Wheat
KISS: Mila Kunis aka Meg from *Family Guy*
MARRY: Mila Kunis aka Meg from *Family Guy*
KILL: Reality TV Shows
DATE: 21/5/2011

SCHOOL REPORT

Pupil name: Stefan Abingdon

Dear Mr K. Abingdon,

I am writing on behalf of myself and my colleagues to inform you that Stefan is becoming a very disruptive individual, a very bad boy indeed. He has become quite attached to one girl in particular, so attached in fact that she has become scared of him. I have been informed he has been freely calling her a 'lesbian', and this will not be tolerated.

I have also become a victim of his abusive behaviour: from stabbing me with foam swords to spraying my face with mace. Yesterday it was Stefan's turn to sing a Christmas ditty to the class and his choice was 'All I Want for Christmas is You'. I was particularly pleased with his choice because this is one of my favourite songs at this time of year – oh how I love Mariah Carey ... However, Stefan went on to change the lyrics in the chorus to 'All I want for Christmas is a fuck buddy'. I was in utter shock to hear such words of filth! This is offensive and rude. If Ms Carey could hear this disgusting language, she would frown upon him too.

Lastly, at any given opportunity, including assembly and school play rehearsals, he feels the need to take off all of his clothes and run around naked. This is not the sort of example I want pupils to set at my school. Address this at once or I will have to take a more serious approach. And while you're at it, please tell him to take his bloody hat off! 'Tis silly.

Yours sincerely,

A.N. Horney
Headmaster

A. N. Horney

E.T. PARODY

Photoshop Master!

POPSTARS TO LITERATI

'You want us to try and write a book?'

At the end of the February tour in 2011 we found ourselves sat in numerous meetings, being presented with the task of writing a Midnight Beast book. We naturally found the prospect of writing a book pretty daunting and I'd be lying if I said I was keen on the idea at first, particularly when we were shown books by N-Dubz, Justin Bieber and S Club 7 as examples of what ours could be like. I guess people thought we were just another boy band! ;-)

We'd almost been turned away from one of the companies we visited when the security guard didn't believe we could possibly be there for a meeting. At that stage we didn't have the author look sussed.

Luckily, we found the company that proved to be right for us. I think it was the big jar of sweets they gave us when we came back for a second meeting that hooked us. Reeled in by the sweets, we found ourselves planning ideas for this so called 'book', pulling out our own favourite books for inspiration. Stef's was the Ali G book, Ashley was particularly fond of Billie Piper's autobiography and I just liked picture books. I still couldn't believe that I was about to part take in writing a book when all we'd been doing before that was basically fucking around for the past year or so! But it was happening and it was time to get out my favourite ~~Parker ink pen~~ laptop.

So after weeks of writing, typing, sweating, laughing and crying we have been delivering different chapters that basically sum up the madness since we became The Midnight Beast.

(Hey look, I even sneaked this in as a chapter, how ironic!)

So Gay

ALL GOOD THINGS MUST COME TO AN END

Stefan

Have you downloaded this book illegally? If so, how the fuck did you manage that, and what's wrong with you? You can literally download anything on the Internet and you've chosen a book? I hope the Internet police catch you.

But seriously, whenever I finish watching a film I always ask whoever I watched it with, 'What was your favourite bit?' I'm not going to ask you that question about this book because I already know the answer: 'All of it.' So I hope you've enjoyed our first text journey, and hopefully it'll be the start of many more. More importantly, I hope you've learnt something ... other than never to buy a book without checking it's a good one first. See you next time, beasts.

Yours sincerely,

Stefan James Donald John
Abingdon

Dru

'And now, the end is near ...'

So here we have it, the ending to The
Midnight Beast's book. I'd like to take this
time to thank you for buying and reading this. That
is, of course, unless you chose to stand there in WH Smith
and read the whole fucking thing so you didn't have to buy it, like
those people do with aeroplane magazines and stuff. I mean let's
face it, it wouldn't have taken long to read this in the shop – it's not
exactly a weighty tome with lengthy chapters and a compelling
protagonist. Nor is there a rather dark twist at the end making
you wonder if there'll be a second volume. Or is the news that
there could be a second the dark twist? Who fucking knows. But
help us out here, I have four kids to feed....

Dru

Ash

Dear Reader,

Well done, you've read a book a child could write. I hope that you take none of our advice or views with so much as a pinch of seriousness. The Midnight Beast has always been a joke and will never be anything more. Who would have thought our homemade videos would land us an E4 series, two sell-out tours, see us headlining a tent at Reading/Leeds, playing Glastonbury and becoming published authors? This has taken us just over a year. Fuck all the haters (I am sure that's the cool thing to say) and thank you to everyone who follows our work. I hope we keep living up to your expectations.

Yours sincerely

Ashley Neil Horne

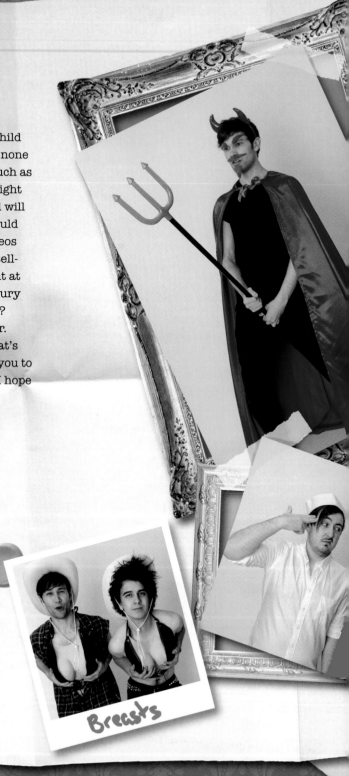

Breasts

oi oi Sailor

SHOUT OUTS

Stefan

Stefan would like to thank mum (for all that t-shirt packing – and for giving birth to me too), dad (for doing every job that I could possibly think of – you're the greatest man alive), Dru and Ashley and their lovely families (for keeping me sane), my brothers Tcha & Kyle (for teaching me all the dirty words I know), my managers/agents/best friends Rachel and Cathy Mason: two fit sisters who are basically the fourth and fifth members of TMB – without them we definitely wouldn't have got this far. Adam and Sam (for ALL the videos you helped us make), Bonnie, Natasha, Grandma, Nana, Viki, Scarlet, Sue, Gary, my boy-friends Simon, Gregg, Chris, Jake, Nick, Pip, Sam, Sam and Tom and all the Hadouken and Chapters boys, our amazing tour-crew Jake, Elliot, Jude, Mark, Josh, Luke, Jack and Guy, Emma over at RMS, Ben, Lee, Stacey, Jade and everybody else at Peter Webber, Kate Maisie, Totally Tom, Doctor Brown, Erika, Selena Gomez, Frank Skinner, Michael Mcintyre, The Ross Family, Felicity and Nick at Curtis Brown, Charlotte and everybody else at Hodder, Nerys, Shane and everybody else at E4, Jason and Joel, Mary and Jen and all the rest at Warp Films and to anybody that I've missed out: thank you as well. Thank you. Bye.

Ash

Firstly I would like to thank my family: Sir Neil Horne, Lady Karen Horne, Duchess Sarah-Louise Horne and the rest of the Horney Horne family... blah, blah, blah. I'd like to thank Stef and Dru, the Abingdons, the Wakelys, Rachel and Cathy Mason (hotties), Felicity Blunt and all the fresh faces at Curtis Brown, Charlotte Hardman (previously known as Haycock) and all the delightful people at Hodder, Nerys Evans, Mary Burke and Jen, Warp films, Jason and Joel, Shane, everyone at E4 comedy, Gregg Chillin, Chris O, Little J, Millen, Tom H, Wayne, Jason, Ben Ellis, Harry Peake, The Ross Family, Michael McIntyre, Frank Skinner, Elliot, Joshyb123, Sir Leon Garner, Nick Hoult, Sylvia Young, Italia Conti, Mimi Schofield, Kanye West, Andrew Sergeant and all my super duper friends. For everyone I missed, I thank you too. Over and Out.

Dru

I would like to thank the whole Wakely family: my mum for giving me my dancing skills, my brother Tim for you all you've done and yes, especially you dad – wherever you may be; my primary school teacher and family friend Miss Wilkins; my Beasts: Stefan – what a musical journey we've been on! – and Ashley – you crazy fucker! – love you guys. I'd like to thank my brothers from another mother: Ashley Gerlach and Reuben 'Tuskah' Douglas; my girlfriend Charlotte; my Drums and Kicks/Clipper Collective Family: Mister E Nigma, Joe Setz, Stuart, Rob, Oli, Nathan; the Abingdon family and the Horne family; Adam Barton and Sam Campbell for helping us with some sick-ass looking videos; Katte Maisie; the Hadouken boys; the talented Gregg and the also talented Chris; Showbiz Simon; the good folk over at Cato music – Sam, you're a legend; everyone at RMS; Ben, Stacey, Lea and all the guys at Peter Webbers; Tina and the Zildjian crew; Totally Tom; Doctor Brown, the good makers of Calpol and of course all of you who actually care for what we do and think we're ever so slightly funny. You're all AWESOME.

Lastly but by know means least I would like to thank all the behind the scenes folk that help us do what we do. Our managers/agents (aka the two fit sisters) Rachel and Cathy Mason who have been utterly amazing and are the reason we are where we are now; the best tour crew ever: Elliot, Jude, Guy, Luke, Stevie, Mark, Josh, Jake, Nick, Kyle and our tour manager Keith; Sally, for all the work in the TMB shop, Felicity, Nick and everyone at Curtis Brown; Charlotte and everyone at Hodder; Mary, Jen and the crew at Warp Films, Nerys and Shane and everybody at E4. And also Jason and Joel – two very, very funny guys! And to anyone one who I have missed out: I'm sorry, it's because I'm... drunk?

Cheers!

And of course
Bell